FROM THE FILMS OF

Harry Potter™

— OFFICIAL —

CHRISTMAS COOKBOOK

FROM THE FILMS OF

Harry Potter

— OFFICIAL — CHRISTMAS COOKBOOK

Text by Jody Revenson
Recipes by Elena Craig

greenfinch

CONTENTS

Introduction 7

Chapter One
BREAKFASTS

Restricted Section Puff Pastry Books 10
Granola Breakfast of Triwizard Champions 12
Snape's Bubble and Squeak 13
Neville's Toad in the Hole 16
*The Chosen One Toast Lightning
Bolts with Coddled Eggs* 18

Chapter Two
SOUPS & STARTERS

Slug Club Christmas Party Spiced Nuts 23
Bubbling Cauldron Bites 25
Swedish Short-Snout's Steak Tartare 27
Yule Ball Prawn Cocktail 29
Slughorn's Appetizer Roll-Ups 31
Nicolas Flamel Vichyssoise Soup 34
Hagrid's One-Pot Pumpkin Stew 36
*Leaky Cauldron's Roasted Tomato Soup with
Marmite Grilled Cheese* 38

Chapter Three
BREADS & SIDES

The Burrow Welcome Wreath 43
Sprout's Superior Sprouts 45
Grimmauld Place Dinner Rolls 48
Sirius Black Hearth Potatoes 51
Weasley Sweater Focaccia 53
Hogwarts Yorkshire Pudding 55

Chapter Four
MAINS

Vegetarian
Greenhouse Greens Salad 59
Madam Pomfrey's Hospitality Shepherd's Pie 60

Meats
'Famous Fire Eaters' Spicy Beef Skewers 63
Marauder's Map Tart 65
Golden Egg Meat Pies 71
Christmas Day Rack of Lamb 73
Christmas Eve Beef Roast 74

Fish & Fowl
Grimmauld Place Roast Turkey Feast 77
Beauxbatons French Fish 80
Yule Ball English Fish Pie 82

Chapter Five
DESSERTS

Giftable Treats

Golden Snitch Popcorn Balls 87
Hagrid's Pumpkin Seed Brittle 89
Every Flavour Cake Pops 91
Ginny's Mini Mincemeat Tarts 95
Great Hall Holiday Fruitcake 99

Cakes & Tarts

Harry's Favourite Treacle Tart 101
Snowy Burrow Cake 103
Sleepy Cupcakes 105
Wizard Chess Pie 107
Butterscotch Ice Cream Pie 109
Great Hall Floating Candle Cake 111

Biscuits

'I'm Sorry, Neville' Biscuit Pops 115
Common Room Jam Sandwich Biscuits 117
Shortbread Christmas Biscuits 118
Golden Trio Biscuits 121

Special Puddings

Professor Trelawney's Pots de Crème 123
Hogsmeade Invisible Snowballs 125
Butterscotch Ice Cream 127
Professor Flitwick's Christmas Figgy Pudding 128
Triwizard Trifle 131

Chapter Six
DRINKS

Hot Chocolate Brooms 137
Hogwarts Punch 139
Durmstrang Punch 141
Beauxbatons Punch 143
Professor Trelawney's Fortified Earl Grey Tea 144
Cast a Christmas Spell Spiced Cider 145
Hair of the Cat 147
Magical Mulled Wine 149
Mistletoe Cocktail 150
Pumpkin Fizz 153
Black Lake Simple Syrup 154
Black and Orange 155
The Grey Lady 156

Chapter Seven
HARRY POTTER HOLIDAY-THEMED PARTIES

Party Planning and Suggested Menus 160
White Erumpent Gift Exchange 161
Yule Ball Party Menu 163
Slug Club Cocktail Party Menu 164
Movie Night Around the Fire 167
Grimmauld Place Christmas Eve Menu 168
Christmas Day Menu 171
Boxing Day Get-Together Menu 172

Glossary 174
Dietary Considerations 175

INTRODUCTION

Christmas in the Harry Potter films is filled with garlands of pine and fir, trees and wreaths decorated with shining gold stars, cards strung on ribbons, flickering candles and ghostly carolers. Traditional Christmas crackers grace tables everywhere, whether at Number Twelve, Grimmauld Place, where the Weasleys enjoy the holiday with Harry and Hermione in *Harry Potter and the Order of the Phoenix*; at the Weasleys' home, The Burrow, in *Harry Potter and the Half-Blood Prince*; or on the tables in the Great Hall in *Harry Potter and the Philosopher's Stone*. When Harry stays at Hogwarts School of Witchcraft and Wizardry during his first year, snow not only falls outside the walls of the castle, but also within the Great Hall, where there are Christmas dinners for the students with bright oranges, tasty roasts and cakes topped with wizard snowmen carrying brooms. It is the gathering of friends and family at Christmas — no matter where and no matter who — and the sharing of a hearty meal and sweet confections that enhances the magic of the holiday.

Inspired by the wizarding world, *Harry Potter: Official Christmas Cookbook* offers everything from soup to nuts for holiday celebrations — Nicolas Flamel Vichyssoise Soup (see page 34) to Slug Club Christmas Party Spiced Nuts (see page 23), of course — as well as hearty main dishes, hot and crusty breads, enchanting desserts and drinks that will raise everyone's spirits. The dishes within this book are inspired by the Harry Potter films, and there are so many even the 30-metre-long tables in the Great Hall might not be able to hold them all. The pumpkin patch on the Hogwarts grounds would be a perfect place to acquire the ingredients for Hagrid's One-Pot Pumpkin Stew (see page 36) or Hagrid's Pumpkin Seed Brittle (see page 89), and the greenhouses outside the castle might grow the vegetables for Sprout's Superior Sprouts (see page 45) or the Greenhouse Greens Salad (see page 59).

Molly Weasley inspired a Weasley Sweater Focaccia (see page 53), and the Divination class's Tessomancy tea cups can be found in Professor Trelawney's Pots de Crème dessert (see page 123). There are Yule Ball dishes that echo the seafood served on screen, and a selection of colourful punches that represent the three schools that compete in the Triwizard Tournament. Drinks include a Magical Mulled Wine (see page 149), Hot Chocolate Brooms (see page 137) and a Mistletoe Cocktail (Nargle-free) (see page 150) for getting warmed up during the cold, wintry days.

No meal would be complete without captivating confections, some inspired by the sweets sold at Honeydukes in Hogsmeade such as Every Flavour Cake Pops (see page 91). Traditional puddings are also included, like Professor Flitwick's Christmas Figgy Pudding (see page 128), a Triwizard Trifle (see page 131) and Harry's favourite dessert — Treacle Tart (see page 101).

Each easy-to-follow recipe lists vegan, vegetarian and gluten-free options with consideration towards everybody's dietary needs. Plus, suggestions are included for easy ingredient substitutions where applicable.

In addition to mouthwatering meals and lip-smacking treats, you'll find ideas for Harry Potter holiday-themed parties and suggested menus for Christmas Eve, Christmas Day and Boxing Day along with ideas for a Slughorn-style cocktail party, a Yule Ball and a Movie Night, among others, to bring about Christmas cheer. The recipes within this book will create unforgettable meals that will give friends, family, partygoers and guests a very Happy Christmas!

BREAKFASTS

Restricted Section
PUFF PASTRY BOOKS

Makes: About 8 pastries
Dietary Notes: V

Over the Christmas holiday of their first year at Hogwarts, Hermione Granger tasks Harry Potter to enter the Restricted Section in the school's library to search for books on Philosopher's Stone creator Nicolas Flamel. These scenes were filmed on location in the Tudor-era Duke Humfrey's Library at Oxford University, which chains its books to the shelves. The books in the Hogwarts Library are thick, heavy tomes that might scream at you when opened, as did the first one Harry looked into during his search. You'll scream in delight at these light and crunchy 'books' made from puff pastry dough.

> 'Good. You can help Harry, then. He's going to go and look in the library for information on Nicolas Flamel.'
>
> 'We've looked a hundred times!'
>
> 'Not in the Restricted Section. Happy Christmas!'
>
> —Hermione Granger and Ron Weasley,
> *Harry Potter and the Philosopher's Stone*

INGREDIENTS

- One 480-g package puff pastry, thawed according to package directions
- 6 tablespoons unsalted butter, melted
- 2–3 drops black food colouring
- 50g sugar
- ½ teaspoon five-spice powder

1. Prepare a baking tray with a silicone baking mat or parchment paper and make sure that the pastry is thawed.
2. Put 2 tablespoons of the melted butter in a small dish and add the food colouring, stir to combine. Have the remaining melted butter in another small dish with two pastry brushes. Mix the sugar with the five spice in a small bowl.
3. Working with one sheet of pastry at a time, roll it out to about 30–25cm. Cut the sheet into 5 by 7.5-cm rectangles, creating 20 from each sheet. Use a 5-cm egg-shaped cookie cutter to cut an egg out of four of the rectangles.
4. Working on the prepared baking tray, place one rectangle down, and brush it with the black butter mixture. Use a fork to prick the centre of the rectangle to make about four rows of marks, and place another rectangle on top. Use the second pastry brush to brush this piece with the plain butter, sprinkle with the spiced sugar and score the centre again with the fork. Layer two more rectangles on top, brushing each with plain butter and sprinkling with more sugar. When you have a stack of four rectangles, take a chopstick and press it down in the centre of the stack, across the short side, creating the centre of the 'book'. Gently indent the top and bottom of the book by pinching with your fingers.
5. Paint the egg-shaped pieces with the black butter and use the tip of the chopstick to create eyes and a mouth. Place this in the centre of the book, pressing gently to adhere. Repeat with the rest of the rectangles and the second sheet of pastry. Leave to chill for 20 minutes in the fridge.
6. While the books are chilling, preheat the oven to 180°C Fan/200°C/Gas 6.
7. Bake for 15–20 minutes or until golden brown and puffed. Serve warm or at room temperature. Store in an airtight container for up to 2 days.

GRANOLA BREAKFAST
of Triwizard Champions

Makes: About 700 g
Dietary Notes: GF*, V, V+*

As we learn in *Harry Potter and the Goblet of Fire*, there are three tasks to be accomplished in the Triwizard Tournament: outwit a dragon, recover a 'treasure' under the waters of the Black Lake, and navigate a dangerous maze in order to win the Triwizard Cup. And as it's said that breakfast is the most important meal of the day, then the tournament's four champions (Durmstrang Institute's Viktor Krum, Beauxbatons Academy's Fleur Delacour and Hogwarts' Cedric Diggory and Harry Potter) would already be front-runners if they started their day with this healthy granola breakfast. Almonds and pecans offer endless energy, oats and flaxseed will fuel the whole body, and the delicious addition of fruits and spices make this a definite winner.

> 'Now, for those of you who do not know, the Triwizard Tournament brings together three schools for a series of magical contests. From each school, a single student is selected to compete.'
>
> —Albus Dumbledore,
> *Harry Potter and the Goblet of Fire*

INGREDIENTS

- 60g coconut oil
- 70g honey or agave
- 190g old fashioned oats
- 60g flaxseed
- 130g whole almonds
- 50g pecan piece
- 1 teaspoon ground cinnamon
- ½ teaspoon ground ginger
- 210g dried fruit combo of choice, such as sultanas, raisins, dried cherries, diced dried apricot and/or coconut flakes

1. Preheat the oven to 130°C Fan/150°C/Gas 2. Line a large baking tray with parchment paper.
2. In a microwave-safe bowl, combine the coconut oil and honey. Heat for 1 minute, carefully remove from the microwave and stir to combine.
3. In a large bowl, combine the oats, flaxseed, almonds, pecan pieces, cinnamon and ginger. Stir together until well combined. Stir the coconut oil and honey into the oat mixture. Spread the mixture onto the baking tray in an even layer and bake for 15—20 minutes, stirring occasionally, until the mixture is mostly dry and the nuts are well toasted.
4. Remove from the oven and stir in your desired dried fruit mixture. Leave to cool completely in the pan. Store in an airtight container for up to 1 month, or package into treat bags as gifts.

Note | This recipe can be made gluten free with gluten-free oats and vegan by using agave instead of honey.

Makes: 6 servings
Dietary Notes: GF, V*

Snape's
BUBBLE AND SQUEAK

Bubble and Squeak, a classic breakfast dish, was named for the sounds made by its ingredients when cooked, which are reminiscent of the gurgles and shrieks made by something brewing in a cauldron in Potions class. Bubble and Squeak is a brilliant way to incorporate any leftovers from Christmas dinner — if there are any! You can mash up any surplus potatoes or root vegetables to use in the recipe. Boxing Day doesn't refer to the sport, but to the boxes of gifts given to those who attended other celebrations on Christmas, and this heartening dish is a gift in itself.

> 'Bubble, bubble, toil and trouble
> Fire burn and cauldron bubble.'
>
> —Frog Choir,
> *Harry Potter and the Prisoner of Azkaban*

INGREDIENTS

- 680g golden potatoes, peeled and cubed
- 120g leftover roasted vegetables, such as Sprout's Superior Sprouts (see page 45) or Quick Roasted Vegetables (see page 74)
- 30g hazelnuts
- 2 tablespoons olive oil
- 6 tablespoons salted butter

1. Bring a large saucepan of salted water to the boil over medium-high heat. Add the cubed potatoes and boil for 10—15 minutes or until the potatoes are tender. Remove from the heat and drain immediately.

2. In a large bowl, mix the hot potatoes with the leftover vegetables, stir to combine and mash well with a wooden spoon or potato masher. Add the hazelnuts and stir again.

3. Add the olive oil and 4 tablespoons of the butter to a large frying pan over medium heat. When the butter is foaming, add the vegetable mixture. Level out in the pan and cook for 10 minutes.

4. Use the flat edge of a wooden spoon to turn over the mixture, scraping up the brown bits from the bottom of the pan and mixing them in, mashing the vegetables a bit more as you go. Level out the mixture again and cook undisturbed for 10 minutes.

5. After the second 10 minutes, stir the mixture again, scraping up all the brown bits and stirring them in. Level the mixture out again, compacting it and shaping it into a thick patty.

6. Cook undisturbed for 20 minutes. Use a spatula to check the bottom to see if it's well browned. If ready, turn off the heat, cover the pan with a large cutting board or platter and flip the patty out of the pan. Serve with fried or scrambled eggs.

Note | This recipe can be made vegetarian by using the Quick Roasted Vegetables instead of Sprout's Superior Sprouts.

The Christmas card–like snow-filled streets of Hogsmeade as seen in *Harry Potter and the Prisoners of Azkaban*.

Neville's
TOAD IN THE HOLE

Makes: 4 servings

Neville Longbottom is constantly losing his toad, Trevor. The warty creature wanders away on the Hogwarts Express before the first-year students enter the Great Hall for sorting in *Harry Potter and the Philosopher's Stone*. Trevor the Toad, played by four different toads in the films, had a terrarium to rest in between takes. The last place he'd be found, however, is in this traditional dish, as there is no record of toads ever being used in the recipe. The name is thought to come from the resemblance of the sausages to the way toads poke their heads out of their burrows.

> 'Has anyone seen a toad? A boy named Neville's lost one.'
>
> —Hermione Granger,
> *Harry Potter and the Philosopher's Stone*

INGREDIENTS

For the Batter
240ml milk
1 tablespoon Worcestershire sauce
1 teaspoon Dijon mustard
3 eggs
130g plain flour
¼ teaspoon salt
Fresh ground pepper to taste

For the Sausages
2 tablespoons vegetable oil
2 tablespoons roughly torn sage leaves
450g sausages

1. Preheat the oven to 180°C Fan/200°C/Gas 6. If possible, do not use a convection oven as sometimes the air flow will inhibit the rising of the Yorkshire pudding.
2. **To make the batter:** In a large measuring jug, whisk together the milk, Worcestershire sauce, mustard and eggs until thoroughly combined. In a separate bowl, stir together the flour, salt and ground pepper. Whisk the egg mixture into the flour mixture until smooth. Set aside to rest.
3. **To make the sausages:** Put a medium cast-iron frying pan, or other high heat pan, on the stove over medium-high heat. Add the vegetable oil, and when it starts to shimmer, add the sage leaves and sausages. Turn the sausages for 2–3 minutes until they brown on all sides. Remove the pan from the heat and remove the sausages to a plate.
4. Pour the batter into the pan and place the sausages on the batter, leaving a bit of space in between each one. Place the pan in the oven. Do not open the oven door for at least 20 minutes. Remove from the oven when dark golden brown and puffed. Serve immediately.
5. Pairs well with scrambled or fried eggs.

Makes: 2 servings
Dietary Notes: V, GF*

The Chosen One
TOAST LIGHTNING BOLTS WITH CODDLED EGGS

When Harry Potter — The Chosen One — was an infant, the Dark wizard Lord Voldemort cast the *Avada Kedavra* curse at him, leaving the baby with a lightning bolt–shaped scar on the right side of his forehead. Over the course of the eight Harry Potter films, Harry's scar was applied to actor Daniel Radcliffe's forehead more than 2,000 times. These coddled eggs bring to mind the first time we see baby Harry in *Harry Potter and the Philosopher's Stone* swaddled in a soft blanket when Dumbledore gently laid him down on the Dursleys' door step. The toasted bread laid on top has its own lightning bolt shape upon it.

INGREDIENTS

2 teaspoons salted butter, plus extra for bread

2 teaspoons grated cheddar cheese

2 eggs

1 tablespoon snipped chives

Fresh ground pepper to taste

2 pieces sliced bread

Speciality Tools

2 egg coddlers or low wide mouth mason jars

Large saucepan with tight-fitting lid and rack or folded tea towel

Lightning bolt-shaped cookie cutter

> 'Do you really have the . . . ?'
> 'The what?'
> 'The scar.'
>
> —Ron Weasley and Harry Potter,
> *Harry Potter and the Philosopher's Stone*

1. **To make the eggs:** Place the rack or folded tea towel inside the large saucepan and place the two empty coddlers or jars inside. Fill the pan with water until it reaches the bottom of the coddler lids. Remove coddlers from the saucepan and bring the water to the boil over medium-high heat.

2. While the water is boiling, use ½ teaspoon of butter on each jar to thoroughly grease the inside of each container. Split the cheese between the bottoms of each jar. Crack the eggs and gently add one to each jar. Top with an additional ½ teaspoon butter each and half the chives each. Add black pepper to taste.

3. Seal each jar or coddler tightly and once the water has reached a boil, place them inside the pan. Cover immediately and reduce the heat to simmer over medium heat. Simmer for 8—10 minutes or until the eggs are set to your desired firmness.

4. **To make the toast:** Butter the centre of both sides of each slice of bread and cut two lightning bolts from each piece. Place in a hot frying pan or on a hot griddle and toast each side to desired doneness. Serve each egg by placing each coddler and two lightning bolts on a salad plate and serve immediately.

Note | This recipe can be made gluten free by using gluten-free bread.

SOUPS & STARTERS

Makes: about 20 servings
Dietary Notes: GF, V

Slug Club Christmas Party
SPICED NUTS

Professor Slughorn's exclusive Slug Club includes a collection of students who are gifted, favourites or expected to go on to illustrious careers. One perk is the Christmas party he hosts, where he serves a variety of his favourite festive hors d'oeuvres: fruit spears, tiny taco shells cradling chopped veggies, pretzels and bowls of nuts. This spiced nut version would fit perfectly at one of his parties and offers a bit of heat with peanuts, cashews and pecans coated with cayenne pepper and garam masala, a warming Indian spice blend.

> 'Everyone, carry on! Carry on!'
>
> —Horace Slughorn,
> *Harry Potter and the Half-Blood Prince*

INGREDIENTS

- 100g light brown sugar, firmly packed
- 1 tablespoon kosher salt
- 1 tablespoon cayenne pepper
- ½ tablespoon garam masala
- 2 egg whites or 4 tablespoons pasteurized egg whites
- 450g roasted, unsalted peanuts
- 450g roasted, unsalted cashews
- 225g roasted, unsalted pecan halves

1. Preheat the oven to 130°C Fan/150°C/Gas 2 and line two baking trays with parchment paper.
2. In a large bowl, whisk together the sugar, salt, cayenne and garam masala. Add the egg whites and whisk until completely combined and a thick paste forms.
3. Add the peanuts, cashews and pecan halves, and stir until they are evenly coated. Spread out the mixture onto the prepared baking trays in even, single layers. Bake for 25–30 minutes, rotating once halfway through, or until the mixture is dry and fragrant.
4. Leave to cool completely before storing in an airtight container for up to 1 week.

Tip | To help break up the nut clusters, roll them up in the parchment while still on the baking tray.

Makes: 12 devilled eggs
Dietary Notes: GF, V

Bubbling Cauldron
BITES

These cauldron-shaped egg bites 'bubble' with chives, peas and horseradish cream, a concoction any potions maker would be proud to produce. For the films, prop makers created more than 200 cauldrons for use in the Potions classes. For Professor Slughorn's classes, three bespoke cauldrons were created in which to hold the potions the professor tests his students with. Hermione Granger identifies the three: one contains Veritaserum, the truth-telling serum; the next is filled with Polyjuice Potion. Then she identifies the love potion Amortentia, which gives off scents unique to the user. The scents she smells that waft up from that particular cauldron are coloured green for 'freshly mown grass', white for 'parchment' and green and orange for 'spearmint toothpaste'.

> 'All students must be equipped with . . . one standard size two pewter cauldron . . .'
>
> —Hogwarts Invitation Letter,
> *Harry Potter and the Philosopher's Stone*

Continued on page 26

INGREDIENTS

6 eggs

120ml rice wine vinegar

3–4 drops black food colouring

75g cooked peas

60ml crème fraîche

1 teaspoon horseradish cream

1 tablespoon snipped chives, plus extra for garnish

¼ teaspoon salt

¼ teaspoon garlic powder

Flat-ended cocktail sticks (optional)

Note | The eggs can be made up to 1 day ahead. Store the egg whites and filling in separate containers and assemble just before serving.

Continued from page 25

1. **To boil the eggs:** Fill a large saucepan, big enough to hold the eggs in a layer, with cold water, until it just covers the eggs. Place the pan on the stove over medium-high heat, cover and bring to the boil. As soon as the water boils, remove the pan from the heat, leave covered, and let sit for 5–6 minutes depending on how firm you like your yolks. While the eggs are cooking, prepare an ice bath in a large bowl. When the eggs are done, submerge them into the ice bath and leave for 2–3 minutes. Peel the boiled eggs.

2. Alternatively, you can use your preferred cooking method or use store-bought hard-boiled eggs.

3. Cut each egg in half across the middle, along the short side. With a paring knife, carefully remove a sliver of egg white so that each half will sit upright.

4. Remove the egg yolk from each half and store in an airtight container in the fridge.

5. Combine the rice wine vinegar and food colouring with 720ml water in a container large enough to hold the eggs in a single layer. Add the egg whites to the container and push each one down so it fills with the dye and place a piece of parchment paper over the top to help them stay submerged. Let the eggs soak in the dye for 5–10 minutes until the desired colour is reached. They should start to resemble small cauldrons.

6. Line a baking tray with a few layers of kitchen paper and use a slotted spoon to remove the eggs from the dye, place them open side down and leave them to dry while you make the filling.

7. To the bowl of a food processor, add the cooked peas, crème fraîche, horseradish cream, chives, salt and garlic powder. Run the processor for about 1 minute until the mixture is mostly smooth. Add the egg yolks and run the processor again for about 30 seconds or until the egg yolks have been incorporated.

8. Set each egg white upright and use a small spoon or cookie scoop to fill each egg with a mounded tablespoon of filling. Garnish with more snipped chives and add a cocktail stick 'spoon' if desired. Serve immediately.

Makes: 4 servings
Dietary Notes: GF*

Swedish Short-Snout's
STEAK TARTARE

Among the variety of starters for Horace Slughorn's Slug Club Christmas Party is a tartare that, unfortunately, does horrible things to one's breath once eaten. (Hermione gobbles some up to keep Cormac McLaggen's unwanted advances at bay.) Inspired by — but not tasting like — that questionable hors d'oeuvre is this tartare featuring filet mignon. This version is great for heating up in cold weather with a blend of dried chilli flakes and wasabi paste in its mix. Even a dragon would enjoy its fiery flavours.

> 'Marvelous creatures, dragons, aren't they?'
>
> —Alastor 'Mad-Eye' Moody,
> *Harry Potter and the Goblet of Fire*

INGREDIENTS

- 225-g filet mignon
- 2 tablespoons finely diced shallot
- ½ teaspoon dried chilli flakes
- ½ teaspoon wasabi paste
- 1 teaspoon lemon zest
- 1 teaspoon kosher salt
- 1½ teaspoons rice wine vinegar
- 1 egg yolk, room temperature
- 2 tablespoons olive oil
- Toasted baguette slices or crackers, for serving

1. Cut the beef into 2.5-cm cubes, cleaning it of any fat or membrane. Place it on a plate and freeze it for 10 minutes.
2. While the beef is in the freezer, in a medium bowl, combine the shallot, dried chilli flakes, wasabi paste, lemon zest, salt, rice wine vinegar and egg yolk. Whisk until blended. Slowly drizzle in the olive oil, whisking as you go, until the dressing comes together.
3. Remove the beef from the freezer and, in small batches, mince it into very small pieces. Fold the beef into the dressing and serve immediately with toasted baguette or crackers.

Note | This recipe can be made gluten-free by serving with a gluten-free baguette or crackers.

Yule Ball
PRAWN COCKTAIL

Makes: 6 servings
Dietary Notes: GF

For the Yule Ball's holiday feast seen in *Harry Potter and the Goblet of Fire*, set decorator Stephenie McMillan decided they should have seafood, served cold on an icy base, complementing the wintry celebration. The Yule Ball was a special occasion for many reasons. It was here Hermione Granger made a fashion statement in a pink ombre dress created from twelve metres of chiffon and silk and a statement in fact that if Ron was jealous of her date, he should have asked her first!

> 'The Yule Ball has been a tradition of the Triwizard Tournament since its inception.'
>
> —Minerva McGonagall,
> *Harry Potter and the Goblet of Fire*

INGREDIENTS

For the Sauce
215g Greek yogurt
55g mayonnaise
1 teaspoon curry powder
½ teaspoon salt
¼ teaspoon cayenne pepper

For the Prawns
450g (about 16—20) raw prawns

1 litre low sodium vegetable broth
1 small lemon, cut in half, plus 2 more, cut into wedges, for garnish
2 bay leaves
1 tablespoon whole peppercorns
2 garlic cloves, peeled and smashed

1. **To make the sauce:** In a 480-ml airtight container, mix together the Greek yogurt, mayonnaise, curry powder, salt and cayenne. Cover and refrigerate for at least 30 minutes, or until ready to serve, to let the flavour develop.

2. **To make the prawn:** Use kitchen scissors to cut along the back of the prawn, leaving the tail intact, and devein. Leave the shells on.

3. In a large saucepan over medium-high heat, add the vegetable broth, lemon halves, bay leaves, peppercorns and garlic cloves. Bring to the boil, turn the heat down to medium-low, add the prawn and cover. Simmer for 3—5 minutes or until the prawn are pink and opaque.

4. Use tongs to move the prawn to a platter. When cool enough to handle, peel and then chill for at least 30 minutes before serving. The prawns can be cooked up to 1 day ahead, refrigerated in an airtight container.

5. When ready to serve, put the sauce in a small bowl in the centre of a platter surrounded by prawn. Garnish with lemon wedges to serve.

Makes: 32 pieces or 8 servings
Dietary Notes: GF, V*, V+*

Slughorn's Appetizer
ROLL-UPS

For his Slug Club Christmas get-together, Horace Slughorn chose to match the party's decorations to the muted red and green tones of the professor's tasselled paisley robe. The space was a redecoration of the Room of Requirement set, whose columns were concealed with layers of a shot silk fabric in jade green. Among the dishes on the red-covered tables are platters of sushi, wrapped in green nori, which gives the effect of Christmas colours.

> 'In the old days, I used to throw together the occasional supper party. Select student or two. Would you be game?'
>
> —Horace Slughorn,
> *Harry Potter and the Half-Blood Prince*

INGREDIENTS

- 380g uncooked sushi rice
- 2 teaspoons rice wine vinegar
- 1 teaspoon salt
- 125g lump crab meat or cooked prawn meat, chopped
- 1 tablespoon mayonnaise
- ½ teaspoon sriracha
- 1 teaspoon dried chives
- ½ teaspoon onion powder
- 4 sheets of nori
- 2 small Persian cucumbers, julienned
- ½ avocado, sliced thin
- 2 teaspoons capers

Speciality Tools
Sushi mat

1. Cook the sushi rice using a rice cooker or according to the package directions. When the rice is cooked, use a rice paddle or flat wooden spoon to spread it out on a baking tray, sprinkle with the rice wine vinegar and salt, and use the paddle to gently fold it in. Once seasoned, spread it out again and set aside.

2. Mix the crab or prawn with the mayonnaise, sriracha, chives and onion powder.

3. Working with one sheet of nori at a time, lay the sheet on the sushi mat with a long side facing you. Use slightly damp hands to spread about a quarter of the rice onto the nori sheet, covering it from edge to edge, leaving a 2-cm border on the edge farthest from you. Place half the seafood mixture down the centre of the rice. Roll the mat away from you once, pressing the filling to create a firm roll. Lift the top of the mat and use your finger to press the clear strip of nori onto the roll. Cover with the mat and roll once more to further tighten the roll. Remove from the mat and set aside.

4. Repeat these steps, first with the remaining seafood, creating a total of two rolls, then with the vegetables, using half the cucumber, avocado and 1 teaspoon of the capers for each roll. When all the rolls are made use a very sharp knife to cut eight equal pieces from each roll. Arrange on a platter and serve immediately.

5. Serve with a small dish of soy sauce if desired.

Note | The filling can be adjusted as needed for either both seafood options, all vegetarian or get creative and choose your own. Smoked salmon, thinly sliced cooked beef or cod roe make great options.

In *Harry Potter and the Chamber of Secrets*, sleighs race over the frozen lake at Christmastime in concept art by Adam Brockbank.

Makes: 6 servings
Dietary Notes: GF, V

Nicolas Flamel
VICHYSSOISE SOUP

Nicolas Flamel is a 665-year-old French alchemist at the time of *Harry Potter and the Philosopher's Stone* and the only known maker of the titular stone itself. Vichyssoise is an American version of a classic French potato-and-leek soup, served cold instead of hot. Though there is only one stone, the prop makers for the film designed several, made out of a moulded resin in a rich ruby red. Harry was surprised to find the stone in his pocket, and you'll be surprised to find a red roasted tomato at the bottom of your bowl the same colour as the Philosopher's Stone.

INGREDIENTS

For the Vichyssoise
4 large leeks
3 tablespoons unsalted butter
1 tablespoon olive oil
1 teaspoon kosher salt, plus more for seasoning
450g golden potatoes, peeled and cubed
1.2 litres vegetable broth
240ml double cream
½ teaspoon ground white pepper

For the Philosopher's Stone Tomatoes
6 vine tomatoes
1 tablespoon olive oil
Up to 1 teaspoon salt

'The only stone currently in existence belongs to Mr. Nicolas Flamel, who last year celebrated his 665th birthday.'

—Hermione Granger,
Harry Potter and the Philosopher's Stone

1. **To make the soup:** Slice the white and light green parts of the leeks thinly, add to a large colander and rinse well.
2. In a large saucepan over medium heat, combine the butter, olive oil and 1 teaspoon salt. When the butter is completely melted, add the leeks. Cook, stirring frequently, for 10–15 minutes until softened but not brown.
3. Add the potatoes and stir to coat, then add the vegetable broth. Increase the heat to medium-high, bring to a low boil, then reduce to a simmer, over low heat. Simmer for 30 minutes or until the potatoes are very tender.
4. Remove from the heat and use a handheld blender to purée for 2–3 minutes or until completely smooth. Add the double cream, white pepper and more salt to taste.
5. **To make the Philosopher's Stone tomatoes:** While the soup is simmering, preheat the oven to 180°C Fan/ 200°C/Gas 6.
6. Place the tomatoes stem side down on a baking tray and coat with the olive oil. Roast for 10–15 minutes or until softened and split. Sprinkle each tomato with a pinch of salt.
7. To serve, place one tomato in the bottom of a low, wide, soup bowl and ladle the soup over it.

Note | Vichyssoise soup can be served hot or cold. Leftovers can be stored in an airtight container for up to 3 days. Roasted tomatoes can be stored in a separate container for up to 3 days.

Makes: 8 servings
Dietary Notes: GF, V, V+

Hagrid's
ONE-POT PUMPKIN STEW

Behind Hagrid's hut is a lush pumpkin patch, the perfect place to find the main ingredient for this nourishing stew, filled with the best of winter's vegetables. The patch was one place his Hippogriff, Buckbeak, rested and where he might have nipped at the vegetables as they grew. The scenes of the pumpkin patch in *Harry Potter and the Prisoner of Azkaban* were filmed on a hillside in the Scottish Highlands. The sitting animatronic Buckbeak was mounted on rails over the muddy turf, as it rained most days while they were shooting. A stew like this one is a great way to brighten up your day, regardless of the weather.

> 'There's no Hogwarts without you, Hagrid.'
>
> —Harry Potter,
> *Harry Potter and the Chamber of Secrets*

INGREDIENTS

- 1 bunch rainbow chard
- 1 tablespoon harissa powder
- One 400-g tin chickpeas, drained
- 2 tablespoons olive oil
- 1 onion, diced
- 2 red peppers, cored, deseeded and diced
- 2 teaspoons salt
- 1.5 litres vegetable broth
- 180g tomato purée
- 680–900g pumpkin or winter squash, such as winter luxury, kabocha or Jarrahdale

1. Tear the leaves from the stems of the chard and set the leaves aside. Rinse the stems and finely dice.
2. In a large saucepan over medium-high heat, add the harissa powder and the chickpeas. Cook for 2–3 minutes, stirring constantly, until the harissa is fragrant and the chickpeas have dried out.
3. Add the olive oil, stir to coat and then add the onion, red pepper and chard stems. Sauté for 2–3 minutes more until the onion begins to soften. Add the salt and continue cooking another 3–4 minutes until the vegetables release their juices and deglaze the bottom of the pan.
4. Add in the vegetable broth and the tomato purée. Stir to combine. Add in the pumpkin chunks and simmer the stew for 20–30 minutes or until the pumpkin is tender.
5. When ready to serve, rinse the chard leaves, roughly chop, stir into the soup and cook for 1 minute. Serve immediately.
6. The stew can be made up to a day ahead and should be refrigerated in an airtight container until serving.

Note | If making the stew ahead, leave the chard leaves out until ready to serve. Reheat the soup, add the leaves, stir and cook for 1 minute.

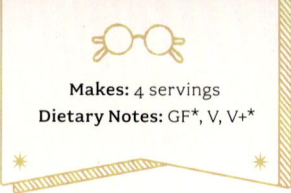

Makes: 4 servings
Dietary Notes: GF*, V, V+*

Leaky Cauldron's
ROASTED TOMATO SOUP
with Marmite Grilled Cheese

A warming roasted tomato soup served with a Marmite grilled cheese sandwich is an iconic British meal that could have been served at The Leaky Cauldron. After all, when you have a cauldron as inspiration, soups are a given. On a sign created by the graphics department for *Harry Potter and the Philosopher's Stone*, there are several soups offered, including Leaky House Soup, Soup Leaky House and House Soup Leaky. This rich tomato soup is accompanied by a grilled cheese sandwich prepared with Marmite, a popular British toast topping, a savoury food spread made from the yeasty byproducts of beer brewing.

INGREDIENTS

For the Soup
900g Roma tomatoes
2 tablespoons olive oil
1 teaspoon kosher salt
1 onion, roughly chopped
3 garlic cloves, peeled and smashed
60ml balsamic vinegar
480ml vegetable broth
120ml unsweetened oat milk

For the Sandwiches
8 slices white or buttermilk bread
3 tablespoons unsalted butter
4 teaspoons Marmite
180g English cheddar, finely grated

> 'Leaky Cauldron! Stay away from the pea soup!'
> —Shrunken head on the Knight Bus, *Harry Potter and the Prisoner of Azkaban*

1. **To make the soup:** Preheat the oven to 200°C Fan/ 220°C/Gas 7 with the rack in the upper third of the oven.
2. Cut the tomatoes in half and remove most of the core and seeds. Place cut side down on a baking tray and coat with 1 tablespoon of the olive oil and the salt. Roast for 15–20 minutes, or until the skin is blistered and the tomatoes are softened.
3. While the tomatoes are roasting, heat a medium saucepan over medium-high heat with the remaining tablespoon of olive oil. Add the onions and garlic and cook, stirring frequently, for 7–10 minutes until the onions are completely soft and starting to brown.
4. Add the balsamic vinegar and use it to deglaze the bottom of the pan. Reduce the heat to low and simmer the onions until most of the liquid has reduced.
5. Add the roasted tomatoes and vegetable broth and simmer for 15–20 minutes until the garlic cloves are very soft and the mixture has thickened slightly.
6. Purée with a handheld blender for about 3 minutes until very smooth. Add the oat milk and stir.
7. The soup should be served immediately or stored in an airtight container in the fridge for up to 3 days.

> **Note** | If you don't have a handheld blender, leave the soup to cool for 30 minutes. Carefully blend in a blender or food processor until smooth. Reheat and stir in the oat milk.

8. **To make the sandwiches:** Cut the crusts off all the bread slices. Spread half the butter evenly across one side of each piece and toast in a large frying pan on medium-high heat until golden brown.
9. Remove from the pan and spread each buttered side with about 1 teaspoon Marmite per sandwich.
10. Place about a quarter of the cheddar cheese on one Marmite side. Top with another piece of bread, Marmite side down. Use the rest of the butter to butter the outsides of each sandwich. Place the sandwiches, one or two at a time, in the pan and grill for about 2 minutes per side until each side is golden brown.
11. Cut each sandwich in half and serve immediately with a bowl of hot soup.

> **Note** | This recipe can be made vegan by using a plant-based spread and cheese. Use gluten-free bread for a gluten-free option.

BREADS & SIDES

Makes: 8—10 servings
Dietary Notes: V

The Burrow
WELCOME WREATH

In *Harry Potter and the Half-Blood Prince*, Harry spends Christmas with the Weasley family at The Burrow, their intricately constructed home. The redheaded family has always given Harry the warmest of welcomes. 'The Weasleys are really the only family Harry's got in terms of love and friendship,' says Julie Walters, who plays the Weasley matriarch, Molly. The love between family members is apparent (although Percy is sometimes on the out) and it's not surprising that they open their home at the holidays to all. This edible Christmas wreath with roasted red pepper 'berries' sends a doughy, pesto holiday greeting to all.

> 'It's not much, but it's home.'
> 'I think it's brilliant.'
>
> —Ron Weasley and Harry Potter,
> *Harry Potter and the Chamber of Secrets*

Continued on page 44

INGREDIENTS

For the Dough
180ml full-fat milk, warmed to 43°C

1 tablespoon sugar

7-g (2¼ teaspoons) instant yeast

400g plain flour

3 tablespoons olive oil, plus more for oiling the bowl

1 egg

1 teaspoon kosher salt

For the Pesto
70g walnut pieces

50g baby rocket leaves

10g basil leaves

¼ teaspoon garlic powder

½ teaspoon kosher salt

2 teaspoons olive oil

For the Wreath Assembly
1 tablespoon olive oil

40g grated parmesan cheese

2 pickled cherry peppers (optional)

2 mini mozzarella balls (optional)

2 rocket leaves (optional)

Note | You can stuff extra peppers with more mozzarella balls and serve in a bowl alongside the bread.

Continued from page 43

1. **To make the dough:** Combine the milk, sugar and yeast in a small bowl. Stir and set aside for 5 minutes until foamy.

2. While the yeast is activating, put the flour, olive oil, egg and salt in the bowl of a stand mixer fitted with a dough hook attachment. Mix on low briefly to combine.

3. Once the yeast is foamy, add it to the stand mixer and mix on low for about 5 minutes until the dough comes together. If the dough is too moist, add 1 tablespoon of flour at a time until it just comes together. Once the dough pulls away from the side of the bowl, continue to knead it with the dough hook for another 5 minutes, until elastic.

4. Place the dough in a large oiled bowl. Cover with a clean towel and leave to rise for 1—1½ hours or until it has doubled in size and is puffy when touched.

5. **While the dough is rising, make the pesto:** Add the walnuts to the bowl of a food processor and pulse 2—3 times. Add the rocket and basil leaves and pulse again until well chopped. Add the garlic powder, salt and olive oil and run the processor for up to 1 minute until a thick paste has formed. Scrape into an airtight container and refrigerate until needed.

6. **To assemble:** Line a baking tray with a silicone baking mat or parchment.

7. Once the dough has risen, roll it out on a lightly floured surface to an approximately 25 x 50cm rectangle. Brush the surface with the tablespoon of olive oil and spread the pesto mixture evenly over the surface. Sprinkle the grated parmesan cheese evenly over the pesto.

8. Starting from a long edge, begin to roll a tight roll and pinch the ends closed. Use a sharp knife to cut the roll in half lengthways. With the filling facing upwards, twist the two pieces together, overlapping alternately, as if you were creating a plait.

9. Gently lift the plait onto the baking tray and form into a circular wreath. Pinch the ends together to close. Pick up any loose filling and sprinkle it back over the wreath using it to cover any exposed dough, especially towards the pinched ends. Cover with greased cling film and leave to proof while you preheat the oven to 180°C Fan/200°C/Gas 6 for about 15 minutes. Bake for 25—30 minutes or until golden brown. Leave to cool for at least 15 minutes before decorating and serving. If decorating, stuff each cherry pepper with a mozzarella ball to 'inflate' and pin onto the wreath with cocktail sticks. Tuck the rocket leaves off to one side.

Sprout's Superior
SPROUTS

Makes: 6 servings
Dietary Notes: GF

Professor Pomona Sprout teaches Herbology at Hogwarts in greenhouses filled with plants of all kinds, which provide ingredients for potions and draughts. Some plants, more than likely, are tasty and nutritional, like the Brussels sprouts in this recipe. To ensure your Brussels sprouts are as superior as Professor Sprout's, remove the thicker outer leaves, which are usually more bitter than other parts of the plant. You should also wash the sprouts to remove any dirt that may be left. In this recipe, bacon offers a splash of salt and dried cranberries add a smidge of sweetness.

> **'Welcome to Greenhouse Three, second years.'**
>
> —Pomona Sprout,
> *Harry Potter and the Chamber of Secrets*

INGREDIENTS

- 450g Brussels sprouts
- 4 pieces of bacon, diced
- 1 tablespoon olive oil
- 35g dried cranberries
- ½ teaspoon salt

1. Preheat the oven to 170°C Fan/190°C/Gas 5.
2. Remove the tough or bruised guard leaves from each Brussels sprout. Rinse the Brussels sprouts in a colander and drain. Cut the tough stem off each one and then cut in half. Set aside.
3. Scatter bacon pieces on a baking tray and bake for 7 minutes, then remove the baking tray from the oven. Add the Brussels sprouts and shake to coat with the bacon pieces. Drizzle with the olive oil. Make sure all the Brussels sprouts are lying cut side down in a single layer. Roast for another 10–15 minutes or until the Brussels sprouts are well browned on the cut edge and tender.
4. Toss with the cranberries and salt. Serve immediately. Save any leftovers in an airtight container and use to make Snape's Bubble and Squeak (see page 13).

The Great Hall covered in silver and ice for the Yule Ball. Concept art by Adam Brockbank for *Harry Potter and the Goblet of Fire*.

Grimmauld Place
DINNER ROLLS

Makes: About 16 rolls
Dietary Notes: V

In *Harry Potter and the Order of the Phoenix*, the Weasley family, Harry and Hermione celebrate Christmas at Number Twelve, Grimmauld Place, the headquarters of the Order of the Phoenix and Sirius Black's ancestral home. A classic holiday spread is prepared, including a plate of rolls —inspiration for this dish — set beside a platter of turkey and potatoes on the long kitchen table. The Black family's six-metre-long kitchen table was handcrafted specifically for the film as tables that long are hard to find! These dinner rolls will also be hard to find once guests bite into these hot and tender baked breads.

> 'Oh, Harry! There you are. Happy Christmas!'
>
> —Molly Weasley,
> *Harry Potter and the Order of the Phoenix*

INGREDIENTS

- 120ml whole milk, warmed to 43°C
- 1 tablespoon honey
- One packet (2¼ teaspoons) instant yeast
- 650g plain flour
- One 400-g tin plain pumpkin purée
- 4 tablespoons unsalted butter, softened, plus more for serving
- 1 egg
- 2 teaspoons kosher salt
- 2 teaspoons paprika
- 1 teaspoon dried rosemary
- Egg wash (1 egg whisked with 1 tablespoon water)
- 2 teaspoons flaked salt (optional)

1. In a small bowl or measuring jug, combine the warmed milk, honey and yeast. Stir to combine and set aside for about 5 minutes until the yeast is foaming.

2. In the bowl of a stand mixer fitted with a dough hook, combine the flour, pumpkin purée, butter, egg, salt, paprika and ½ teaspoon of dried rosemary. Mix briefly to combine and then add the yeast and milk mixture and continue to mix.

3. Once a shaggy dough forms, stop the mixer and scrape down the sides of the bowl. Continue to knead with the dough hook on low for 5 minutes. Once the dough pulls away from the side of the bowl and becomes elastic, transfer it to a large oiled bowl, cover with a clean towel, and leave it to rise for 1—1½ hours, or until the dough has doubled in size.

4. While the dough is rising, line two baking trays with a silicone baking mat or parchment paper.

5. Working on a lightly floured surface, separate the dough into 16 equal portions. Working with one portion at a time and lightly floured hands, roll the dough out into a long snake, about 40cm in length. Create a knot by forming a loose circle, in one hand, with a long tail. Use the other hand to feed the tail in and out of the circle and bring the end up through the middle. Place each finished knot on a prepared sheet. Leave to proof for about 1 hour until they are puffy. Towards the end of proofing, preheat the oven to 170°C Fan/190°C/Gas 5.

6. Before the rolls go in the oven, brush each one with the egg wash and sprinkle with a few leaves of the remaining dried rosemary. Bake until golden brown and the internal temp reaches 88°C. Remove from the oven and sprinkle each roll with a pinch of flaked salt, if using. Serve warm with more softened butter.

Sirius
BLACK HEARTH POTATOES

Makes: 6 servings
Dietary Notes: GF, V, V+*

Messages in the wizarding world can be sent by owl post, by Patronus and by portraits. But what about a face-to-face conversation through the coals of a fireplace? Yes, that's possible, too. Harry Potter and Sirius Black have one such exchange in the Gryffindor common room's massive fireplace during the winter in *Harry Potter and the Goblet of Fire*. The common room was the first warm, comforting experience Harry has had outside his cupboard under the stairs, and these potatoes are also as comforting as time spent relaxing on the plush red couches in front of the common room's blazing fire. These delicious, tender potatoes are completely covered in a combination of black lava salt and kosher salt, then baked in a cast-iron pan to emerge from an ashy crust.

> 'Meet me in the Gryffindor common room at one o'clock this Saturday night.'
>
> —Letter from Sirius Black,
> *Harry Potter and the Goblet of Fire*

INGREDIENTS

- 680g new or fingerling potatoes
- 240g kosher salt
- 2 sprigs rosemary
- 30g black salt
- 2 tablespoons unsalted butter (optional)

1. Preheat the oven to 170°C Fan/190°C/Gas 5.
2. Wash the potatoes well and dry them.
3. In a cast iron or ovenproof frying pan, make a base layer of half the salt. Arrange the potatoes in a single layer on top of the salt layer. Tuck in the two sprigs of rosemary around the edge of the pan.
4. Mix the remaining salt with the black salt. Pour the salt mixture evenly over the potatoes. They should be mostly covered but not necessarily completely covered.
5. Bake for 45—60 minutes or until the skins on the potatoes are puffed and the potatoes are fork tender.
6. Use a fork or tongs to remove the potatoes from the salt. Serve as is or toss with 2 tablespoons unsalted butter.

Note | Once the salt has cooled, it can be saved to bake more potatoes, to serve as pie weights or to use as a scrub for pots and pans. This recipe is easily made vegan by omitting the butter.

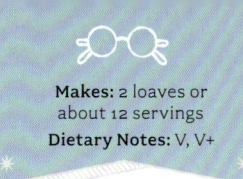

Makes: 2 loaves or about 12 servings
Dietary Notes: V, V+

Weasley Sweater
FOCACCIA

Given that the set designer and prop makers considered the Weasleys' home to be drafty, it's not surprising that Molly Weasley knits a lot of clothing for her family. And at Christmastime, it's likely her gifts will be made by her crafty hands. Over time, each of her children has received a sweater with their initial on the front, as seen in *Harry Potter and the Philosopher's Stone*. Harry gets one as well during his first year at Hogwarts. These Italian flatbreads, called focaccia, have monogram toppings for Harry and Ron baked in, but feel free to get creative and add your own monogram.

> 'What are you wearing?'
> 'Oh, my mum made it. Looks like you've got one, too!'
>
> —Harry Potter and Ron Weasley,
> *Harry Potter and the Philosopher's Stone*

Continued on page 54

Continued from page 53

1. In a medium bowl or measuring jug, combine the water, sugar and yeast. Set aside for about 5 minutes until foamy.

2. In a large bowl, combine the flour and salt. Once the yeast is foamy, add it to the flour mixture and use a rubber spatula to stir it until no dry flour remains and a shaggy dough has formed.

3. Pour 4 tablespoons of the olive oil into a very large bowl, add the dough and turn it two to three times to coat it with olive oil. Cover with a clean tea towel or cling film. At this point the dough can either go in the fridge overnight, or to a warm place for 4 hours. The dough is ready when it has doubled in size.

4. When the dough is ready, deflate it by keeping the dough in the bowl and using two forks to flip the edge farthest from you towards you. Turn the bowl a quarter turn and repeat this step. Turn the bowl two more times, using the forks to flip the dough each time. You should be creating a rough ball.

5. Pour 2 tablespoons olive oil onto each baking tray, or 4 on the larger tray, if using, and turn and tilt the pans to coat with the oil. Split the dough in half and place on the baking trays. Pour any remaining olive oil from the bowl onto each loaf. Let the dough proof in a warm place for about 1½ hours until doubled in size. It is ready when an indent, made with the tip of your finger, bounces back slowly and leaves a mark. If it bounces back quickly it needs more time. Towards the end of proofing, preheat the oven to 210°C Fan/230°C/Gas 8.

6. When the dough is done proofing, gently push it to the edges of the trays with your fingers and then make dimples all over with the tips of your fingers.

7. Decorate with the vegetables and/or fruit creating an R monogram in the centre of one loaf and an H monogram in the centre of the other (or whatever monogram you'd like). Drizzle each with 1 tablespoon olive oil and sprinkle with ½ teaspoon salt, if using. Bake for 25—30 minutes or until golden brown all over and crisp at the edges. Serve warm. Leftovers can be stored in an airtight container for up to 3 days.

INGREDIENTS

600ml water, warmed to 43°C

2 teaspoons sugar

1 packet (2¼ teaspoons) instant yeast

680g plain flour

1 tablespoon kosher salt

150ml olive oil

500g berries or diced vegetables (see note)

1 teaspoon flaked salt (optional)

Speciality Tools

Two 23-by-33-cm (or one 43-by-23-cm) baking trays

Note | Peppers, spring onions, red onions, shallots or finely diced carrots work well as vegetable décor. Sliced strawberries, blueberries, raspberries or thinly sliced pears work well for fruit options. Make sure to use a good-quality olive oil that you love the taste of because it will feature prominently in the final product.

Makes: 12 puddings
Dietary Notes: V*

Hogwarts
YORKSHIRE PUDDING

As there are four houses at Hogwarts School of Witchcraft and Wizardry, there are four ingredients needed to make the traditional British Yorkshire pudding: eggs, flour, milk and some form of fat that can range from oil to beef drippings. We generally think of 'pudding' as being synonymous with dessert, but it can also refer to cake-like dishes such as this crispy puffed bread. Yorkshire puddings originated from York in Northern England.

INGREDIENTS

- 4 eggs
- 240ml full-fat milk
- ½ teaspoon salt
- 130g plain flour
- 60ml pan drippings from roast beef (or high temperature oil, such as grape seed or avocado oil) (see note)

1. Add the eggs to a large bowl and whisk thoroughly. Add the milk and salt and whisk again. Add the flour all at once and whisk vigorously for up to 3 minutes until no lumps remain and the batter is smooth. Leave the batter to rest for at least 30 minutes.
2. Preheat the oven to 210°C Fan/230°C/Gas 8.
3. Place 1 teaspoon of pan drippings into each cavity of a muffin tin. Heat the pan and oil in the oven for 10 minutes. While the pan is heating, transfer the batter to a jug.
4. Remove the pan from the oven. Pour the batter over a spoon to prevent splashing and fill each cavity ⅔ full. Bake for about 20—25 minutes or until golden brown and crisp. Do not open the oven while baking until at least 20 minutes has gone by, as this may prevent rising. If possible do not use a convection oven as this may prevent rising.

> 'Welcome, welcome to another year at Hogwarts. Now, I'd like to say a few words before we all become too befuddled by our excellent feast.'
>
> —Albus Dumbledore,
> *Harry Potter and the Prisoner of Azkaban*

Note | Pan drippings from roast beef area classic for Yorkshire Pudding but if your drippings fall short of 60 ml, you can top them off with a high heat oil or replace the beef drippings altogether for a vegetarian option.

MAINS

Makes: 6 servings
Dietary Notes: GF, V, V+*

Vegetarian

Greenhouse Greens
SALAD

In *Harry Potter and the Chamber of Secrets*, second-year students file into Greenhouse Three for their first Herbology lesson, in which Professor Pomona Sprout teaches them how to repot the problematic, screaming baby Mandrakes. More than fifty animatronic Mandrakes were created for the scene, squirming and wriggling in their pots via controllers who sat under the Greenhouse's massively long trestle table. It's much less difficult to make this mouthwatering salad for a hearty dinner, which combines a crop of wintry vegetables including squash and rainbow carrots, plus fruity pomegranates, for a burst of colour and lip-smacking flavour.

> 'Professor Sprout tells me you have an aptitude for Herbology.'
>
> —Alastor Moody to Neville Longbottom,
> *Harry Potter and the Goblet of Fire*

Note | This recipe can be made vegan by substituting maple syrup or agave for the honey.

INGREDIENTS

For the Salad
- 1 squash
- 2 teaspoons olive oil
- 2 rainbow carrots, peeled
- 1 cucumber, peeled
- 4 radishes, cleaned and sliced thin
- 60g pomegranate seeds
- 170g cherry tomatoes
- 170g dry quinoa, cooked according to package directions
- 70g walnuts
- 150g salad leaves

For the Dressing
- 120ml olive oil
- 60ml balsamic vinegar
- ½ teaspoon kosher salt
- ½ tablespoon Dijon mustard
- 1 tablespoon honey
- 30g finely minced shallot

1. **To make the salad:** Preheat the oven to 180°C Fan/200°C/Gas 6.
2. Cut the squash in half lengthways, scrape out the seeds and pulp and cut into 1-cm slices to create crescent moons.
3. Place the slices on a baking tray and toss with the olive oil. Roast for 10—15 minutes, or until tender and browning. Leave to cool on the baking tray while making the rest of the salad.
4. While the squash is roasting, make the dressing: In a bowl or measuring jug, add the olive oil, vinegar, salt, mustard, honey and shallot. Whisk until the dressing emulsifies. Set aside until ready to dress the salad.
5. **To assemble the salad:** Have a large salad bowl standing by. Use a vegetable peeler to cut wide ribbons of carrot into the salad. Stop when you reach the core of the carrot and save for a soup stock or discard.
6. Cut the cucumber in half lengthways and scrape the seeds out with a spoon. Cut into 1-cm slices and add them to the bowl.
7. Add the radishes, pomegranate seeds, tomatoes, walnuts, cooled squash and quinoa. Toss all the ingredients together with the dressing, giving it a quick whisk again if needed. Add the salad leaves and toss again. Serve within 1 hour.

Makes: 6 servings
Dietary Notes: GF, V

Vegetarian

Madam Pomfrey's Hospitality
SHEPHERD'S PIE

Madam Poppy Pomfrey is the matron at Hogwarts, the 'school nurse' who offers kindness to injured or bespelled students, whether they need to regrow bones, be restored from being Petrified by a Basilisk or have been bitten by a possible Grim. Though she's no-nonsense, Madam Pomfrey is also gentle and calming, like the best comfort food. Shepherd's Pie is a traditional Irish dish that dates back to the 1700s. It's typically made with meat, but it's the simmered leeks, onions, mushrooms and roasted cashews topped by fluffy mashed potatoes that give this its cozy flavour.

INGREDIENTS

For the Mashed Potatoes
1.1kg gold potatoes, peeled and cubed
120g cream cheese
4 tablespoons salted butter
1 teaspoon salt
Fresh ground pepper to taste

For the Filling
480ml vegetable broth
120g roasted unsalted cashews
2 tablespoons vegetable oil
4 tablespoons salted butter
1 small leek, thinly sliced
1 small onion, diced
225g cremini mushrooms, thinly sliced
2 tablespoons tapioca starch

> 'He should have been brought straight to me! I can mend bones in a heartbeat, but growing them back...'
>
> —Poppy Pomfrey,
> *Harry Potter and the Chamber of Secrets*

1. **To make the potatoes:** Bring a large saucepan of salted water to the boil over medium-high heat. When the water is boiling, add the potatoes, bring the water back to the boil, turn down the heat to medium-low and simmer for 10–15 minutes or until the potatoes are very tender.
2. Drain the potatoes and return them to the pan. Put the pan back on the hot burner but with the stove off, and mash the potatoes with a potato masher until most of the steam has released. Add the cream cheese and butter and continue to mash and stir until the dairy has melted and everything is well combined. Add the salt and fresh ground pepper to taste. Set aside while making the filling.
3. **To make the filling:** Preheat the oven to 170°C Fan/190°C/Gas 5.
4. In a small saucepan or microwave-safe measuring jug, heat the vegetable broth for about 1 minute to scalding. Remove from the heat and add the cashews. Set aside.
5. Add the vegetable oil and butter to a large sauté pan over medium heat. When the butter begins to foam, add the leek and onion. Sauté for 3–4 minutes until the vegetables are softened, then add the mushrooms. Continue to sauté for 5–7 minutes until the mixture begins to brown. Sprinkle with the tapioca starch, stir to combine and cook for 2 more minutes, stirring slowly. Add the broth and cashews and use the liquid to deglaze the bottom of the pan. Simmer for 2–3 minutes until the mixture thickens slightly.
6. Pour the filling mixture into a deep pie dish or casserole dish and spread the potatoes over the top. Bake for 25–30 minutes or until the potatoes puff and begin to brown.

'Famous Fire Eaters'
SPICY BEEF SKEWERS

Makes: 4 servings as a main, or up to 8 as an appetizer
Dietary Notes: GF

Meats

Harry Potter sneaks into Hogwarts Library's Restricted Section searching for information on Philosopher's Stone creator Nicolas Flamel during Christmas break in *Harry Potter and the Philosopher's Stone*. He reads aloud a few titles in the 'F' section starting with *Famous Fire Eaters* before opening a book where a screaming face bulges out from the pages. The Restricted Section scenes were filmed in Oxford University's Bodleian Library, the oldest reading room at Oxford. *Famous Fire Eaters* could offer one way of grilling these extra fiery beef delights, spiced with chipotle peppers, garlic and ginger, but it's much easier to use a grill or your oven.

> 'Famous Fire Eaters. Fifteenth Century Fiends. Flamel, Nicolas Flamel. Where are you?'
>
> —Harry Potter,
> *Harry Potter and the Philosopher's Stone*

Tip | If preparing as a main, the skewers can be served over rice or pasta coated in the pepper sauce.

INGREDIENTS

- 2 red peppers
- 1 tablespoon grapeseed or avocado oil
- 1 bunch coriander leaves
- 450g flank steak, cut into thin strips about 2.5cm wide
- 1½ teaspoons salt
- Juice of 2 limes
- 3 black garlic cloves, peeled
- 4 tablespoons whole chipotle peppers (from a can of chipotle peppers in adobo)
- 10cm piece of ginger, peeled and cut into large chunks
- 1 tablespoon olive oil
- 1 tablespoon rice vinegar

Speciality Tools
Skewers

1. Preheat the oven to 210°C Fan/230°C/Gas 8.
2. Slice each pepper in half and remove the seeds and membranes. Place on a baking tray and rub with the grapeseed oil. Roast, cut side down, for 20 minutes or until blistered and softened. Remove from the oven and set aside until the peppers are cool enough to handle. Once they are cool, peel the skin from each pepper piece, discard and set the peeled peppers aside.
3. Remove any wilted or bruised pieces from the coriander bunch and rinse the rest well. Chop the stems away from the leaves, as close as you can get to the leaf top as possible. Set the leaves aside.
4. In a medium well-sealed container, mix the steak pieces, 1 teaspoon of the salt, lime juice, 2 tablespoons of the chipotle pepper that are mostly sauce, the coriander stems, black garlic and ginger pieces. Seal the container and shake well to coat and blend everything. Transfer to the fridge to marinate for at least 1 hour or up to 4.
5. While the meat is marinating, make the sauce. In the bowl of a food processor, combine the roasted red pepper pieces, the coriander leaves, the remaining ½ teaspoon salt, the olive oil and the rice vinegar. Purée in the food processor for about 1–2 minutes until smooth. Refrigerate until serving.
6. When ready to cook the meat, heat a grill or oven and baking tray to 170°C Fan/190°C/Gas 5. While preheating, soak 12 skewers in water for 5 minutes. When the skewers have soaked, remove them from the water and thread one to two strips of beef onto each skewer, catching it in several places, like a ribbon. Sear on each side for 1 minute and cook for about 3–4 minutes more, turning halfway through. Serve with the sauce for dipping.

Makes: 8 servings

Meats

Marauder's Map
TART

To allow Harry Potter to join his classmates for a winter's trip into Hogsmeade, twins Fred and George Weasley gift him the Marauder's Map, originally created by four Hogwarts students. The map shows the location of everyone in the castle and secret passageways out of the castle leading to other places such as Honeydukes sweet shop (take the one-eyed witch passageway) or the Shrieking Shack, both in Hogsmeade. The ingredients in this savoury dish evoke the Marauders — the Animagi Padfoot (Sirius Black), Prongs (James Potter) and Wormtail (Peter Pettigrew) — who protected their lycanthropic fourth member, Remus Lupin, at the full moon. The tart is topped by a Whomping Willow fashioned from the same dough as the crust, hiding the tart's hearty meat, cheese and vegetable assortment, just as it hid an entrance into the Shrieking Shack where the Marauders met.

> 'Messrs. Moony, Wormtail, Padfoot & Prongs are proud to present the Marauder's Map.'
>
> —James Potter, Sirius Black, Remus Lupin, Peter Pettigrew, *Harry Potter and the Prisoner of Azkaban*

Continued on page 66

Continued from page 65

INGREDIENTS

For the Crust
325g plain flour
1 teaspoon salt
60g unsalted butter, very cold
30g solid vegetable shortening, very cold
About 80ml ice water
1 egg
¼ teaspoon ground nutmeg
Fresh ground pepper

For the Filling
125g pancetta, diced
70g sliced mushrooms
90g baby spinach leaves, packed
100g grated gruyère cheese
2 slices prosciutto, cut into ribbons
480ml double cream
3 eggs
½ teaspoon sumac
Black pepper to taste

1. **To make the crust:** In a large bowl, combine the flour and the salt. Cut the butter and shortening into tablespoon-sized pieces and add to the flour mixture. Use a pastry cutter or two forks to cut into the flour. Add the water a little bit at a time and mix gently until the dough comes together.

2. Split the dough in half and roll out one half to fit a 23-cm pie dish with at least 1-cm overhang. Trim any excess dough from around the edge until you have an even 1-cm overhang, fold under and crimp as desired. Refrigerate for 30 minutes. Preheat the oven to 180°C Fan/200°C/Gas 6.

3. Roll out the second half of the dough and use a pastry cutter or paring knife to cut a rough tree shape, a rounded top over a thick trunk. Transfer the dough to a baking tray lined with a silicone baking mat or parchment paper. Cut into the rounded top creating three thick branches. Plait the three branches together once. Use the pastry cutter again to cut smaller branches from the top of each large branch. Twist and bend the branches to resemble the leafless Whomping Willow in the winter. Chill on the baking tray for at least 30 minutes.

4. After the crust has chilled, line it with 2 pieces of overlapping aluminium foil to cover the bottom and the edges. Fill with baking beans or dried beans and bake for 10 minutes.

5. While the crust is baking, in a small bowl whisk the egg with 1 tablespoon water. Remove the crust from the oven, remove the foil and baking beans and use a fork to prick the bottom and sides of the crust. Use a pastry brush to coat the bottom and sides of the crust with the egg wash. Return the crust to the oven and bake for another 7–10 minutes or until golden brown. Remove from the oven and set aside.

6. Brush the willow with the egg wash, and sprinkle with the nutmeg and a few turns of fresh ground pepper. Bake for 10–15 minutes or until crisp and golden brown. Remove from the oven and set aside.

7. **To make the filling:** Reduce the oven temperature to 170°C Fan/190°C/Gas 5.

8. In a medium frying pan over medium-high heat, add the pancetta and sauté for 2–3 minutes until most of the fat has been rendered. Add the mushrooms, stir to coat and continue to cook for another 3 minutes until the mushrooms soften and begin to brown. Add the spinach leaves, stir to combine and cook for 1 minute until the spinach is barely wilted.

9. Add the mixture to the bottom of the cooked pie shell. Top with the gruyère cheese and then top with prosciutto ribbons.

10. Add the cream, eggs, sumac and pepper to a large bowl, whisking until well combined. Pour over the filling. Bake for 30–35 minutes or until set at the edges but with a bit of jiggle in the middle.

11. Leave to cool for at least 10 minutes before serving. Top with the baked Whomping Willow.

Note | The tart can be served warm, room temperature or cold. It can be stored in an airtight container for up to 3 days.

Harry, Ron, and Hermione visit Hogsmeade, which is permanently above the snowline, in *Harry Potter and the Prisoner of Azkaban*. Concept art by Andrew Williamson.

Makes: About 12 pies or 6 servings

Meats

Golden Egg
MEAT PIES

For the first task of the Triwizard Tournament, Harry must capture a golden egg that, once opened, offers a clue necessary to completing the second task. Graphic designer Miraphora Mina, who devised the look of the golden egg, emphasized the idea of discovery as she planned the prop. Mina wanted Harry to break through the egg to uncover what was inside. Similarly, once your fork or fingers open these golden 'eggs', you'll discover the sweetness of Italian sausage combined with tangy winter apples and fennel in a delicious triumph of tastes.

> 'Come seek us where our voices sound, we cannot sing above the ground. An hour long you'll have to look, to recover what we took.'
>
> —The Merpeople's clue for the second task, *Harry Potter and the Goblet of Fire*

Continued on page 72

Continued from page 71

INGREDIENTS

For the Filling
450g mild Italian sausage
100g chopped fennel
1 medium onion, diced
1 crisp apple, cored and diced
½ teaspoon salt

For the Crust
650g plain flour
1 teaspoon kosher salt
2 teaspoons turmeric
225g vegetable shortening, cold
225g unsalted butter, cold
80ml ice water
1 egg, for egg wash

Speciality Tools
Egg-shaped cookie cutter
Other small cookie cutters, such as leaves

1. **To make the filling:** In a large frying pan over medium-high heat, brown the sausage for about 5 minutes until almost no pink is seen. Using a slotted spoon, transfer the sausage to a plate and set aside.

2. To the same pan, add the fennel and onion, stirring to coat in the fat. Sauté for 2—3 minutes, stirring occasionally. Add the apple and salt, stir to combine and continue to cook for another 3—5 minutes until softened and beginning to brown. Remove from the heat and mix with the sausage. Set aside to cool while making the dough.

3. **To make the crust:** In a large bowl, combine the flour, salt and turmeric. Cut the butter and shortening into tablespoon-sized pieces and add to the flour mixture. Use a pastry cutter or two forks to cut into the flour. Add the water a little bit at a time and mix gently until the dough comes together.

4. **To assemble:** Line two baking trays with silicone baking mats or parchment paper.

5. On a lightly floured work surface, working with ¼ of the dough at a time, roll out the dough until about 5mm thick. Use the cookie cutter to cut out 24 egg shapes, and reserve the scraps for decoration.

6. Lay out six dough eggs on each baking tray. Top each egg with about 20g filling, keeping it in the centre. Cover the filling by gently stretching a second egg and placing it over the top of the filling. Use a fork to crimp the edges closed. With your fingers, gently indent the crimp edging towards the egg in spaced intervals to create a more decorative edge. When all the eggs have been assembled, roll out the scraps and use small cookie cutters to cut decorative shapes, such as leaves.

7. Mix the egg with 1 tablespoon water to create an egg wash. Brush each pie with the egg wash. Use a metal straw or a sharp knife to create a vent and add the decorations. Brush egg wash onto each decorative piece. Chill in the fridge while preheating the oven to 180°C Fan/200°C/Gas 6. Bake for about 25—30 minutes or until the pastry is crisp and golden brown. Leave to cool for 10 minutes before serving.

8. Store leftovers in the fridge for up to 4 days. The pies can be reheated in an oven preheated to 160°C Fan/180°C/Gas 4 for 10 minutes.

Christmas Day
RACK OF LAMB

Makes: 4 servings
Dietary Notes: GF

Meats

Feasts at Hogwarts are iconic scenes in the Harry Potter films, featuring flavoursome vegetable dishes such as ears of corn and mashed potatoes, brightly coloured fruits and mouthwatering main dishes, among them racks of lamb dripping with juices. Another variation is the crown rack of lamb, seen at the Hogwarts Welcome Feast, called such because its circular construction topped with paper frills (called manchettes) resembles a crown. If it was served at Christmastime, it wouldn't be the only crown on the table. Set decorator Stephenie McMillan always placed Christmas crackers on the table during holiday scenes. These traditional hollow toys include a paper crown to be worn by the partygoers.

> 'Find a broomstick in your stocking,
> See the magic on display,
> Join the owls' joyous flocking,
> On this merry Christmas Day.'
>
> —Hogwarts Ghostly Carolers,
> *Harry Potter and the Philosopher's Stone*

INGREDIENTS

- 8 chops or 1.1kg rack of lamb
- 1 teaspoon salt
- Fresh ground pepper to taste
- 2 tablespoons Dijon mustard
- 2 tablespoons olive oil
- 2 teaspoons balsamic vinegar
- 1 teaspoon dried mint
- ¼ teaspoon dried chilli flakes
- 60ml cooking sherry
- 120ml vegetable broth (optional)

1. With a rack centred in the oven, preheat the oven to 200°C Fan/220°C/Gas 7. Remove the lamb from the fridge about 30 minutes before cooking. Trim the excess fat blanket by starting at the thicker side and using a sharp knife to slice the fat along the meat and away from it. Once you have a section freed you should be able to pull the rest off in one piece (a thin fat layer remaining is fine). Rub the lamb with the salt and pepper to taste. Set aside. In a small bowl, combine the mustard, olive oil, vinegar, mint and dried chilli flakes and whisk to emulsify. Set aside.

2. Place a large ovenproof frying pan over medium-high heat for 1–2 minutes. Place the lamb meat side down and sear for about about 2 minutes until well browned. Use tongs to flip to the other side and sear for another 2 minutes. Pour off any fat drippings from the pan and discard. Use a pastry brush to cover the entire lamb rack in the mustard mixture, making sure to coat the ends.

3. Place the rack bone side down in the pan, add the sherry to the bottom of the pan and roast in the oven until the internal temperature of the centre chop reaches 52°C for rare and 54°C for medium-rare. Remove from the oven, and tent with foil for 5–10 minutes before serving.

4. When ready to serve, use a carving knife to cut between the chops and serve 2 chops to each person. Serve with Quick Roasted Vegetables (see page 74), Sprout's Superior Sprouts (see page 45) and/or Sirius Black Hearth Potatoes (see page 51).

5. If you want to make a quick pan sauce, rest the lamb on a cutting board tented with foil. Skim most of the fat from the pan and return it to the stove over medium heat. Add the vegetable broth and bring it to a simmer, deglazing the bottom of the pan. Serve each pair of chops with a spoonful of sauce.

Makes: 8 servings
Dietary Notes: GF

Meats

Christmas Eve
BEEF ROAST

A beef roast has been the most traditional of holiday feasts since the mid-1800s, typically accompanied by potatoes and other roasted root vegetables such as Brussels sprouts (try Sprout's Superior Sprouts on page 45) and plum pudding. A boneless eye roast is one of the less expensive cuts you can use for this roast; others are beef tenderloin, ribeye or prime rib. This succulent roast might have been served at the Christmas Eve feast for students remaining at Hogwarts over the holiday, which included the Weasley siblings and Harry Potter in *Harry Potter and the Philosopher's Stone*. Wearing their iconic initialed sweaters, the Weasleys enjoyed Christmas Eve in the Great Hall, which was lined with pine trees decorated with crescent moons, stars and orbs, each topped by a large gold star.

INGREDIENTS

For the Beef
One 1.5–2kg boneless eye roast
1 tablespoon kosher salt
1 teaspoon black ground pepper
1 teaspoon dried thyme
1 tablespoon vegetable oil

For the Pan Gravy
120ml red wine
1 tablespoon salted butter
1 tablespoon tapioca starch
240ml vegetable broth

For the Quick Roasted Vegetables
540g mixed root vegetables such as carrot, parsnip, turnip, or bite-size new potatoes
2 tablespoons olive oil
½ teaspoon kosher salt

'**Let the feast begin!**'

—Albus Dumbledore,
Harry Potter and the Philosopher's Stone

1. **To make the roast:** Place the meat in a shallow dish or airtight container and rub all over with the salt, black pepper and thyme. Tightly cover with a lid or cling film and transfer to the fridge for at least 4 hours or up to overnight.
2. Preheat the oven to 90°C Fan/110°C/Gas ¼.
3. In a large ovenproof frying pan over medium-high heat, add the vegetable oil and when it begins to shimmer, add the roast. Sear the roast on all sides for 4—5 minutes per side. Use tongs to hold the roast steady when searing the ends and narrow sides.
4. Roast in the oven for 1—1½ hours, or until the meat reaches an internal temperature of 46°C.
5. Turn the oven off, leaving the roast in the oven with the door closed, for an additional 30—40 minutes. Remove the meat from the oven when the internal temperature reaches 52°C. Transfer the roast to a cutting board or serving platter, tent with foil and leave to rest for 20 minutes while making the pan gravy.
6. **To make the gravy:** If making Hogwarts Yorkshire Pudding (see page 55), reserve 60ml of drippings.
7. Add the red wine to the pan with the beef drippings over medium-high heat, and deglaze the pan, stirring and cooking the wine for 2—3 minutes.
8. Add the butter, stir until melted and then sprinkle the tapioca starch over the mixture. Whisk until it forms a thick paste. Whisk in the vegetable broth and leave to simmer for 3—5 minutes until thickened.
9. **To make the Quick Roasted Vegetables:** While the roast is resting, preheat the oven to 170°C Fan/190°C/Gas 5.
10. Scrub the vegetables clean and cut into uniform pieces about 5cm in size.
11. On a large baking tray, toss all the vegetables with the olive oil and salt and shake out to a single layer. Roast for about 20—25 minutes or until fork tender and browned.

Makes: 12—15 servings
Dietary Notes: GF*

Fish & Fowl

Grimmauld Place
ROAST TURKEY FEAST

The Weasleys, Harry Potter and Hermione Granger spend the Christmas holiday with Sirius Black at his home, Number Twelve, Grimmauld Place, in *Harry Potter and the Order of the Phoenix*. Molly Weasley put together a superb feast: dinner rolls, silver tureens more than likely filled with a bready stuffing and tasty vegetables, a large roast turkey with crispy brown skin and a side of gravy on the six-metre-long custom-made table made by the prop makers. Turkey arrived on British shores in the 1500s and became part of the Christmas table — King Henry VIII is thought to be an early patron of this popular holiday meal.

> 'Have a wondrous wizard Christmas,
> Have a merry Christmas Day.
> Move around the sparkling fire,
> Have a merry Christmas Day.'
>
> —Hogwarts Ghostly Carolers,
> *Harry Potter and the Philosopher's Stone*

Continued on page 78

Continued from page 77

INGREDIENTS

For the Brine

500g kosher salt

2 tablespoons black peppercorns

1 tablespoon dried herbs of choice, such as sage, thyme, oregano and/ or rosemary

5½–6¾kg fresh turkey, giblets and neck removed

For the Stuffing

680g lightly packed bread cubes (see note)

340g mushrooms of preference

1 onion

1 bunch of celery, outer stalks removed

450g bulk sausage

2 tablespoons unsalted butter, plus more for greasing

1–1½ litres low sodium vegetable broth

2 tablespoons salted butter (optional)

For Roasting the Turkey

6 tablespoons unsalted butter

Turkey lacing kit

Speciality Tools

Brining bag or large pan big enough to hold the turkey and space in the fridge or a large cooler filled with ice

Large roasting pan with a V-rack

---

1. **To make the brine:** Fill a large pan with 4 litres water and add the salt, peppercorns and desired herb combination.

2. Heat over medium-high heat, stirring until all the salt is dissolved. Remove from the heat and add 4 litres ice water. Stir until the ice melts and refrigerate the mixture until it is completely cool.

3. If using a brining bag, place the turkey, breast side down, in the bag and rest in a roasting pan for support. Fill the bag with the cooled brine mixture and seal well. Place in the fridge or cooler and brine for at least 30 minutes per 450g, or up to 1 hour per 450g. If using a pan, place the turkey, neck end down, and pour in the brine, cover and proceed as above.

4. **To make the stuffing:** Preheat the oven to 100°C Fan/ 120°C/Gas ½ and spread the bread cubes out in single layers on two baking trays (you may need to work in batches to toast all the bread). Let the bread toast in the oven for 20 minutes, then turn the oven off and leave to cool. This can be done up to 3 days ahead. Store the bread in an airtight container or plastic bag.

5. Thinly slice the mushrooms and set aside. Dice the onion and the celery, using the whole heart and leaves, and set aside, keeping separate from the mushrooms.

6. In a large frying pan over medium-high heat, add the sausage to the pan and brown for 5–7 minutes, breaking up into small pieces with a wooden spoon. When the sausage is brown, use a slotted spoon to remove the meat to a plate and set aside.

7. Add the butter to the same pan and when it begins to foam, add the mushrooms. Sauté the mushrooms, stirring occasionally, for 2–3 minutes until they are starting to brown. Add the onion and celery and continue to cook, stirring to combine for another 3–5 minutes until the celery and onion are softened. Remove from the heat and transfer to a very large bowl, add the sausage to the vegetable mixture and stir to combine.

8. Add the bread cubes and stir to combine. Start to add the vegetable broth, 240ml at a time, until the mixture is well moistened and starts to hold together. Transfer about a third of the stuffing to a greased casserole dish.

9. If stuffing the turkey, continue to add broth to the remaining stuffing until it is quite wet but still holds together. Use the wetter stuffing to stuff the cavities of the turkey.

10. Press the stuffing into an even layer in the casserole dish, cover with foil and refrigerate until needed. To heat and serve, preheat the oven to 160°C Fan/180°C/Gas 4 and bake, covered, for 30 minutes. Uncover, dot with the salted butter, if desired, and continue to bake until the centre temperature reads 74°C.

11. **To roast the turkey:** Place the oven rack to lowest position and preheat the oven to 140°C Fan/160°C/Gas 3.

12. Remove the turkey from the brine, rinse it and pat it dry with paper towels. If stuffing the bird, loosely fill the cavities with stuffing and truss closed. Using a pastry brush, brush the turkey skin all over with the melted butter. Add 240ml water to the bottom of the pan.

13. Place the turkey, breast side down, on the roasting rack in the roasting pan. Roast breast side down for 2 hours, basting once with the pan drippings.

14. After 2 hours, remove the turkey from the oven and using silicone oven mitts or thick stacks of paper towel for each hand, grab the turkey at both ends and turn it breast side up. Baste with more pan drippings and return to the oven. Roast for another 1–1½ hours or until the thigh temperature reaches 80°C and, if used, the stuffing in the centre of the bird reaches 74°C.

15. Remove the turkey from the oven, tent with foil and leave to rest for 20 minutes before carving. Serve with the stuffing, Quick Roasted Vegetables (see page 74), Sprout's Superior Sprouts (see page 45) and/or Sirius Black Hearth Potatoes (see page 51).

Note | For the bread cubes you can use a variety of breads and it is wonderful to mix them. Sourdough, black bread, multigrain or even loaves with nuts and dried fruit can add fantastic texture to the stuffing.

To make this recipe gluten-free, you can use store-bought gluten-free stuffing mix or substitute gluten-free bread cubes.

Makes: 2 servings as an main or 6 as an appetizer
Dietary Notes: GF

Fish & Fowl

Beauxbatons
FRENCH FISH

Perhaps the women of Beauxbatons Academy of Magic would have enjoyed having this French-inspired oyster-based main dish served at the Yule Ball; it would certainly match the other shellfish on the menu. With a classic combination of French flavours such as apple, fennel and shallots, this stands out like the French blue of the Beauxbatons students' outfits. This dish can be served either cold and raw, or cooked and hot. Fleur Delacour and her classmates might have preferred the warmer version, as costume designer Jany Temime purposely chose a light silk fabric for their costumes, wanting them to appear inappropriately dressed for Hogwarts' cool Scottish weather.

> 'The champion from Beauxbatons Academy—
> Fleur Delacour!'
>
> —Albus Dumbledore,
> *Harry Potter and the Goblet of Fire*

INGREDIENTS

- 4 tablespoons white balsamic vinegar
- ½ teaspoon salt, plus more for the oysters
- ½ teaspoon sugar
- ½ green apple, peeled, cored, and diced
- 2 tablespoons finely minced shallot
- 1 tablespoon finely minced fennel, with fronds if possible
- 12 small fresh oysters

1. In a small bowl, combine the vinegar, salt and sugar, and stir to dissolve. Add in the apple, shallot and fennel and stir again. Leave to sit at room temperature for 30 minutes to let the flavours meld. If not using after 30 minutes, store in an airtight container in the fridge for up to 3 days.

2. When ready to serve, scrub the oysters and discard any that remain open. Shuck the oysters and place them on an oyster platter or regular serving dish with a bed of salt. Place about 1 teaspoon of sauce on each oyster and have the rest available in a small dish with a spoon.

3. If you're not a fan of raw oysters, here is a cooked version: Preheat the oven to 130°C Fan/150°C/Gas 2.

4. Scrub the oysters, discarding any that remain open, and place them on a baking tray.

5. Bake for 3—5 minutes until they just pop open.

6. While they are baking, add 2 tablespoons unsalted butter to a small sauté pan over medium heat. When the butter begins to foam, add the apple-vinegar mixture and sauté for 2—3 minutes until most of the liquid has absorbed. Remove from the heat and set aside.

7. Remove the oysters from the oven and set the grill to high. Open each oyster and free the meat from its shell, nestling it back inside. Top each oyster with about 2 teaspoons apple mixture and grill for 2—3 minutes or until the apple mixture begins to brown. Serve immediately.

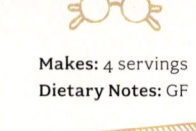

Makes: 4 servings
Dietary Notes: GF

Fish & Fowl

Yule Ball
ENGLISH FISH PIE

The classic English Fish Pie dates back to the 1600s, and became a piscatory alternative to Shepherd's Pie, named 'Fisherman's Pie' as it substituted fish for lamb under its creamy mashed potato crust. Seafood was served at the Yule Ball in *Harry Potter and the Goblet of Fire*, though as a cold dish, not a hearty hot one. The set decoration team went to London's famous fish market, Billingsgate, for their main course. You needn't go so far, as this dish is all about doing things easily.

INGREDIENTS

For the Mashed Potatoes
- 680g gold potatoes, cubed
- 2 tablespoons unsalted butter
- 45g grated Parmesan cheese
- Salt and freshly ground pepper, to taste

For the Pie Filling
- 1 tablespoon olive oil
- 1 tablespoon salted butter
- 2 carrots, diced
- 4 spring onions, white and light green parts, thinly sliced
- 2 garlic cloves, diced
- 120ml double cream
- 450g cod, haddock or white sea bass
- 45g parsley leaves, packed, roughly chopped
- Juice and zest of 1 lemon
- ½ teaspoon salt

'Blimey, Harry, you slay dragons. If you can't get a date, who can?'

'I think I'll take the dragon right now.'

—Ron Weasley and Harry Potter,
Harry Potter and the Goblet of Fire

1. **To make the potatoes:** Bring a large saucepan of salted water to the boil over medium heat. Add the cubed potatoes. Bring back to the boil and simmer over medium heat for 10–15 minutes, or until the potatoes are very tender.
2. Drain the potatoes and return them to the hot pan. Place the pan on the stove, and with the burner off, mash the potatoes gently until most of the steam has been released. Add the butter and half the Parmesan cheese and stir until the butter is melted. Continue to stir briskly until the potatoes are light and fluffy. Taste, and adjust the seasoning with fresh ground pepper and salt. Set aside until needed.
3. **To make the filling**: Preheat the oven 170°C Fan/ 190°C/Gas 5.
4. In a medium frying pan over medium-high heat, add the olive oil and butter. When the butter begins to foam, add the carrots, spring onions and garlic. Sauté for about 3 minutes until the vegetables are tender.
5. Add the cream and continue cooking and stirring for 3–5 minutes until the cream reduces and thickens. Pour into a 23-cm-by-23-cm casserole dish and set aside.
6. Cut the fish into 2.5-cm chunks, looking carefully for and removing any pin bones. In a medium bowl, mix the fish with the parsley, lemon zest, lemon juice and salt. Scatter the fish mixture over the vegetable mixture in the casserole dish.
7. Using a soup spoon, scoop the mashed potatoes on top of the fish in big dollops, covering the surface. Gently spread each dollop with the back of the spoon to create a scale pattern. Sprinkle the remaining Parmesan cheese over the top. Bake for 20–25 minutes, or until brown and bubbly. Leftovers can be stored in an airtight container for 24 hours.

DESSERTS

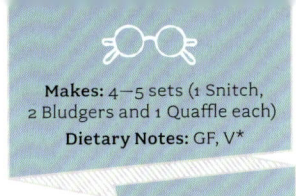

Makes: 4–5 sets (1 Snitch, 2 Bludgers and 1 Quaffle each)
Dietary Notes: GF, V*

Giftable Treats

Golden Snitch
POPCORN BALLS

Harry Potter becomes the youngest Seeker in a century at Hogwarts when he's recruited to play for the Gryffindor Quidditch team in *Harry Potter and the Philosopher's Stone*. A Seeker's responsibility is to catch the Golden Snitch, a small ball that darts around like a hummingbird worth 150 points when caught, ending the game. Several designs were considered for the Golden Snitch's wings to give it credible aerodynamics but the wings on these won't need to fly far — only into your mouth as a sweet holiday treat. Other balls in the game are Bludgers, hit by Beaters to distract players, and the Quaffle ball, which scores points when thrown through a hoop, also represented in this recipe.

> 'The only ball I want you to worry about is this . . . the Golden Snitch.'
>
> —Oliver Wood,
> *Harry Potter and the Philosopher's Stone*

INGREDIENTS

- 135g popped popcorn (about 150g of kernels)
- 1 tablespoon water
- 330g golden syrup
- 40g mini marshmallows
- 280g icing sugar
- ½ teaspoon salt
- 60g unsalted butter, plus more for greasing hands
- 100g gold sanding sugar
- 2 tablespoons black cocoa powder
- 25g cocoa powder
- 160g white chocolate chips (optional)
- 10 wooden cocktail sticks (optional)
- Gold lustre dust, optional

Continued on page 88

Continued from page 87

6. **To decorate:** Pour the sanding sugar into a shallow bowl and roll each snitch in the sugar to coat completely. Set aside (extra sugar can be reused).

7. Place the black cocoa powder into a separate shallow bowl and working above the bowl use a pastry brush to dust the entire surface of each bludger. Repeat with a clean bowl, the cocoa powder and the quaffles.

8. **To make the wings for the snitches:** In a microwave-safe bowl, melt the white chocolate in 30 second bursts for a total of 1 minute. Stir until smooth. Lay a piece of parchment paper on a flat work surface. Using a narrow carving knife, coat the top 7.5cm of the knife on one side in a thick layer of chocolate. Press the tip of the knife against the parchment and draw the knife toward you smearing the chocolate like you would paint on a palette, creating a feather shape. Place a cocktail stick in the centre of the feather leaving about 1cm exposed. If needed, spread a bit more chocolate over the cocktail stick to cover. Use the tines of a fork to gently scrape the 'feathers' into the chocolate, working from one side to the other, being careful not to go all the way through. Repeat the process, making sure to pull the fork the opposite direction to create a mirrored wing. Continue until you have enough sets of wings. Leave the wings to set for 5 minutes.

9. Once the wings are set, carefully remove them from the parchment and hold with the cocktail stick. Gently brush both sides with gold lustre dust. Insert the wings into the snitch popcorn balls just before serving, using the exposed cocktail stick end.

1. Line 2 baking tray with silicone baking mats or parchment paper. Have extra softened butter standing by for greasing hands. Place the popped popcorn in a very large bowl.

2. Add the water, golden syrup, marshmallows, icing sugar, salt and butter to a medium saucepan. Bring to the boil over medium heat, stirring continuously, until all the marshmallows are melted and the mixture is smooth.

3. Remove from the heat and pour over the popcorn, stirring quickly to combine. Make sure to incorporate all the syrup mixture, scraping it off the bottom of the bowl. Leave to sit for 1—2 minutes.

4. Using buttered hands, create the snitches by using about 2 tablespoons of the popcorn mixture and shaping it into a tight ball. Place on one of the baking trays. Next create pairs of bludgers, by using about palm-sized lump of the mixture, shape into tight balls of equal size and place on a baking tray. You will need to regrease your hands periodically.

5. To create the quaffles, use a slightly larger amount of the mixture. Form tight balls, as above, but once formed hold the ball in your two hands and use your thumbs and pointer fingers to create the signature indentations. Make three deep dents in the 'sides' of the ball and 2 shallow indents, one on the top and one on the bottom. Place on the baking trays.

Note | The chocolate wings are very fragile so you will want to make extra sets. If a sturdier set of wings is desired there are many premade paper ones available online. Just make sure to inform guests the wings are décor only and not edible. This can be made vegetarian by using vegetarian marshmallows.

Hagrid's
PUMPKIN SEED BRITTLE

Makes: About 570g
Dietary Notes: GF, V

Giftable Treats

It's not just the flesh inside a pumpkin that can be used to make sweet or savoury dishes — pumpkin seeds can be used for any number of snacks and desserts, and it wouldn't be surprising for someone like Hagrid to utilize every part of the pumpkins he grows in his garden. Though peanut brittle is a Southern American confection, it has been adapted around the world, and this pumpkin seed version is highly nutritious — and delicious.

> 'I've got presents?'
>
> —Harry Potter,
> *Harry Potter and the Philosopher's Stone*

INGREDIENTS

- 300g sugar
- 160g golden syrup
- 150ml water
- 280g roasted salted pumpkin seeds
- 1 tablespoon unsalted butter, plus more for greasing
- 1 teaspoon bicarbonate of soda
- 1 teaspoon vanilla extract
- 2 teaspoons coarse finishing salt

1. Grease a baking tray with butter.
2. Place the sugar, golden syrup, water and pumpkin seeds in a 2-litre microwave-safe bowl. Cook on high/maximum power for 7 minutes. Carefully remove from the microwave, place on a heatproof surface, and gently stir to combine.
3. Cook again on high/maximum power for 15—17 minutes or until syrup separates into threads. This is the hard-crack candy stage or 150°C on a sugar thermometer. While this is cooking, measure out the butter, bicarbonate of soda and vanilla into separate small bowls, and have standing by.
4. Once the nuts and syrup reach the hard-crack stage, carefully remove from the microwave, as above, and stir in the butter, bicarbonate of soda and vanilla just until light in colour and bubbly.
5. Pour onto the buttered baking tray on a heatproof surface, and spread in a thin layer. Sprinkle finishing salt across the entire surface while warm. Leave to cool completely and break into pieces. Store in an airtight container at room temperature for up to one week.

Makes: 16 cake pops
Dietary Notes: V

Giftable Treats

Every Flavour
CAKE POPS

At their first Christmas together, in *Harry Potter and the Philosopher's Stone*, Ron munches on a box of Bertie Bott's Every-Flavour Beans while he watches Harry open his presents. These cake pops evoke this popular wizarding candy, imitating its red, white and yellow packaging, which was created by graphic artists Miraphora Mina and Eduardo Lima. Every cake pop has a bean on top. Consumers will have to guess which pop to dare to have, for not all the beans are sweet — the candy also features other flavours such as earwax or bogies. Will the inside have a matching flavourful yummy bean or the opposite?

> 'They mean every flavour. There's chocolate and peppermint, and there's also spinach, liver and tripe.'
>
> —Ron Weasley,
> *Harry Potter and the Philosopher's Stone*

Continued on page 92

Continued from page 91

INGREDIENTS

400g cake crumbs (about half Triwizard Trifle cake recipe (see page 131)

55g cream cheese, softened

2 tablespoons butter, softened

40g white chocolate chips, melted

85g Bertie Bott's Every Flavour Beans

570g white melting chocolate

150g red candy melts

150g yellow candy melts

Speciality Tools

16 lollipop sticks

2 small, clean craft brushes

1. In a large bowl, combine the cake crumbs, cream cheese and butter. Use a hand mixer fitted with paddle attachments on low to mix until a dough starts to come together. Scrape down the sides of the bowl and add the melted chocolate. Mix again on medium until all the ingredients are homogenous and the dough begins to pull away from the sides of the bowl.

2. Line a baking tray with a silicone baking mat or parchment paper. Sort out the beans: decide how many 'surprise' cake pops you will have. Match flavours together creating 16 pairs. For the surprise pops, create pairs with similar colours, such as Green Apple and Grass or Marshmallow and Earwax.

3. In a microwave-safe bowl, melt about 30g of the white melting chocolate for 30 seconds, and stir until smooth.

4. Using about 2 tablespoons of the cake mixture, form a cake pop and place it on the lined baking tray. Repeat with the remaining cake mixture. Dip the end of each lollipop stick in the melted chocolate and then push the stick about 2.5cm into each cake pop. Press a bean into the side of each pop making sure it is well secured but still visible. Set the matching/paired beans aside. Transfer the cake pops to the freezer for 1 hour.

5. Towards the end of the freezing time, melt the remaining white chocolate in a microwave-safe bowl in 30 second bursts. Stir until smooth.

6. Working with 1 cake pop at a time, note the bean inserted into the cake, find its mate and then dip the pop in the chocolate. Make sure to cover the whole pop, up to the stick, shake off excess chocolate and place back on the baking tray. Immediately press the matching bean into the chocolate. Repeat with the remaining cake pops.

7. Leave the cake pops to set for 5–10 minutes.

8. Add the candy melts to two separate small bowls, and microwave in 30-second bursts for 1 minute. Stir until smooth. Use small, clean craft brushes to paint red and yellow stripes on the cake pops. Leave to set 5 minutes.

9. Once set, the cake pops can be stored in an airtight container in a cool dry place for up to 3 days. Or wrap in cellophane bags as gifts.

Makes: About 12 tarts
Dietary Notes: V

Giftable Treats

Ginny's Mini Mincemeat TARTS

Mincemeat pies, in any size, are integral to a British Christmas. And while they did start out in the Middle Ages with minced mutton or beef, they shifted to the fruit and candied peel version in Victorian times. English tradition maintains that when combining the mincemeat ingredients, one should stir in a clockwise direction and make a wish. In *Harry Potter and the Half-Blood Prince*, Ginny feeds Harry a tiny tart like these during the holiday at the Weasleys', and that turned out very well.

> **'Open up, you.'**
>
> —Ginny Weasley to Harry Potter,
> *Harry Potter and the Half-Blood Prince*

Continued on page 96

Continued from page 95

INGREDIENTS

For the Mincemeat
1 lemon, for zest and juice
2 crisp apples, peeled, cored, and chopped
2 teaspoons unsalted butter
200g dark brown sugar, firmly packed
60ml apple juice
130g sultanas
130g currants
30g candied ginger, diced
2 teaspoons orange marmalade
¼ teaspoon ground clove

For the Pastry
340g plain flour
1 teaspoon salt
2 teaspoons icing sugar
½ teaspoon ground cinnamon
115g unsalted butter, very cold
60g solid vegetable shortening, very cold
80ml ice water

Speciality Tools
12 hole muffin tin
8.5-cm round cookie cutter or pastry wheel
A 5-cm star or round cookie cutter

1. **To make the mincemeat:** Zest the lemon and set the zest aside in a small bowl. In a medium saucepan, combine the apples, butter and the juice of the lemon, and cook over medium heat for about 5 minutes until the apples soften. Add the brown sugar and the apple juice and continue to cook for another 5—7 minutes until all the sugar is dissolved.

2. Add the sultanas, currants, ginger, marmalade and clove and stir until well combined. Continue to cook for about 10 minutes until the mixture thickens enough to coat the back of a spoon. Transfer to a bowl, add the lemon zest, and leave to cool completely before filling the tart shells.

3. **To make the pastry:** In a large bowl, combine the flour, salt, icing sugar and cinnamon. Cut the butter and shortening into tablespoon-size pieces and add to the flour mixture. Use a pastry cutter or two forks to cut into the flour. Add the ice water a little bit at a time and mix gently until the dough comes together.

4. Grease the cavities of the muffin tin well with butter. Roll out half the pastry dough to about 3mm thick. Use the cookie cutter to cut out 8.5-cm circles and press gently into the bottom of each muffin tin cavity. Keep the sides as straight as possible and make sure the dough goes all the way to the bottom of the tin. Use the tines of a fork to crimp the edges of each tart shell. Refrigerate the tin with the tart shells.

5. Roll out the second half of dough and cut out 5-cm stars or rounds, transfer to a baking tray and refrigerate for at least 15 minutes. Preheat the oven to 170°C Fan/190°C/Gas 5.

6. Fill each cavity with about 3 tablespoons filling, top with a pastry star or circle and bake for 20—25 minutes until the filling is bubbly and the pastry is golden brown. Leave to cool in the pan for 15 minutes before using an offset spatula to remove them from the tin. Leave to cool completely on a wire rack before storing in an airtight container between layers of parchment paper. These can be kept at room temperature for up to 3 days.

A starry winter night outside the Burrow, the home of the Weasley family, in concept art by Andrew Williamson for *Harry Potter and the Half-Blood Prince*.

Makes: Three 15-cm cakes
Dietary Notes: V

Giftable Treats

Great Hall Holiday
FRUITCAKE

Christmas cake is packed with seasonal dried fruits such as cherries and apricots that give it sweetness and flaked almonds that add a tasty texture. Fruit and nut cakes became extremely popular in the British Isles during the Middle Ages. It's not surprising, then, that this would be served at a feast at Hogwarts as the school was founded in the middle of the Middle Ages. A touch of brandy will make eating this as cozy as sitting at one of the 30-metre-long Great Hall house tables in front of the massive fireplace.

> 'Ding dong, ding dong,
> Ring the Hogwarts bell!'
> —Hogwarts Ghostly Carolers,
> *Harry Potter and the Philosopher's Stone*

Continued on page 100

Continued from page 99

INGREDIENTS

65g sultanas

65g dried cherries, diced

150g dried apricot halves, diced

360ml brandy

225g salted butter, plus more for greasing

300g dark brown sugar, firmly packed

100g granulated sugar

4 eggs, separated

160g flaked almonds

340g plain flour, plus more for the pans

1 teaspoon baking powder

½ teaspoon salt

½ teaspoon nutmeg

½ teaspoon allspice

Speciality Tools

Three 15-cm cake tins

Three 38-by-38-cm pieces of muslin

Three 38-by-38-cm pieces of foil

1. In a large container with a tight-fitting lid, combine the sultanas, cherries and apricots. Cover with half the brandy, stir to combine, cover and leave to soak overnight at room temperature.
2. Drain the fruit over a bowl, reserving the fruit and the liquid.
3. Grease the cake tins with butter, line the bottoms with rounds of parchment paper and flour the sides. Preheat the oven to 115°C Fan/135°C/Gas 1.
4. In the bowl of a stand mixer, beat the butter for 1 minute until light and fluffy. Add the brown sugar and granulated sugar a little at a time. Continue mixing until well blended.
5. Add the egg yolks, one at a time, mixing after each addition and scraping down the sides of the bowl.
6. In a medium bowl, combine the almonds with 65g of the flour and set aside. In another medium bowl combine the remaining flour with the baking powder, salt, nutmeg and allspice.
7. Add half the flour mixture to the butter mixture and mix until well combined. Add the reserved fruit liquid and mix again, scraping down the sides of the bowl. Add the remaining flour and mix until well combined. Set aside.
8. In another bowl, using the stand mixer or a hand mixer, beat the egg whites until stiff peaks form. Fold the egg whites into the batter, followed by the fruit and then the nuts. Split the batter evenly between the three tins. Bake for 1—1½ hours or until a skewer inserted in the centre of the cake comes out clean and the cake is golden brown. Leave to cool in the pan for 15 minutes before using an offset spatula to gently separate the edges of the cake from the tin and inverting onto a cooling rack. Flip again and cool right side up.
9. When the cakes are completely cool, soak the pieces of muslin in the remaining brandy. Lay down a piece of foil, cover it with a piece of soaked muslin and place a cake in the centre. Wrap the cake, first in the muslin and then in the foil. Repeat with the remaining cakes.
10. Store the cakes in the fridge for up to 3 months. The cakes can be eaten immediately but are best made at least a month ahead to let the flavours develop and the brandy soak in. If making a month or more ahead, check the cakes every two weeks, and if the muslin is dry, spritz with more brandy and rewrap.
11. When serving, the fruitcake can be decorated with dried fruits and nuts and even tied with a ribbon.

Harry's Favourite
TREACLE TART

Makes: 8 servings
Dietary Notes: V

Cakes & Tarts

Treacle tart is a quintessential teatime — or anytime — dessert and known to be a favourite of Harry Potter. Treacle is a byproduct of the sugar-making process and comes in both light and dark varieties. This recipe uses golden syrup, the lighter form of treacle, combined with lemon and breadcrumbs to make a custard-like filling that has the added sweetness of chocolate chips.

> 'Happy Christmas, Harry.'
> 'Happy Christmas, Ron.'
>
> —Ron Weasley and Harry Potter,
> *Harry Potter and the Philosopher's Stone*

INGREDIENTS

½ recipe pastry from Wizard Chess Pie (see page 107), but substitute ½ teaspoon of ginger for cinnamon

Zest and juice of 1 lemon

330g golden syrup

2 eggs

75g fresh white breadcrumbs

80g milk chocolate chips

Whipped cream, for serving (optional)

Speciality Tools

23-cm loose bottom tart tin or ceramic tart tin

1. On a lightly floured surface, roll out the dough and fit it to your tart tin. If using a loose bottom tin, trim the dough with the edge of the tin by pressing the overhang against the edge. If using a ceramic tin, use a sharp knife to trim the edge. Chill for 30 minutes.
2. Towards the end of the chilling time, preheat the oven to 200°C Fan/220°C/Gas 7.
3. Once chilled, line the pastry shell with foil and fill with baking beans or dried beans. Bake for 10 minutes.
4. Remove from the oven, remove the foil and weights and prick all over the bottom and side with a fork. Return to the oven for 10 minutes.
5. While the pastry is baking, prepare the filling by adding to a large bowl the lemon juice and zest, golden syrup and eggs. Whisk together until well blended. Add the breadcrumbs and fold in until well combined.
6. Remove the pastry shell from the oven and scatter the chocolate chips on the bottom. Leave to stand for 5 minutes.
7. Pour in the filling, level it out and bake for 20—25 minutes until golden brown and set, but still with a bit of jiggle in the middle. Leave to cool on a wire rack. The tart can be served warm or cold. Serve with whipped cream if desired.

SNOWY BURROW CAKE

Makes: 8—12 servings
Dietary Notes: V

Cakes & Tarts

Harry spends Christmas at The Burrow in *Harry Potter and the Half-Blood Prince*, where the holiday table is set with golden Christmas crackers, mismatched china and a cake topped with tall, tree-shaped peaks of white frosting (and a figure-skating snowman). This sponge cake swaps in snowmen-shaped truffles for a topper. The Weasley home is quirky, playful and warm. Set designer Stephenie McMillan wanted the house to appear that most everything in it was bought in second-hand shops or rescued from discarded rubbish. The house itself was made to seem as if Arthur Weasley built it all.

> 'Ding dong, ding dong,
> Make the Christmas morning bright.
> Fly high across the sky,
> Light the Christmas night.'
> —Hogwarts Ghostly Carolers,
> *Harry Potter and the Philosopher's Stone*

INGREDIENTS

For the Cake Batter
3 eggs
240ml full-fat milk
Zest of 1 small orange
2 tablespoons fresh orange juice
1 teaspoon vanilla paste or vanilla extract
300g plain flour
250g caster sugar
4 teaspoons baking powder
¼ teaspoon salt
170g salted butter, softened

For the Truffles
180g white chocolate
60ml whipping cream
¼ teaspoon orange extract
¼ teaspoon ground ginger
Cornflour, for dusting hands
180g white candy melts or additional white chocolate (see note)
Gummy sweets, liquorice and hundreds and thousands (optional)

For the Frosting and Filling
340g white chocolate
500g cream cheese, softened
275g unsalted butter, softened
2 tablespoons orange juice
1 teaspoon vanilla extract
70g orange marmalade
4—6 pretzel sticks (optional)
Large open star nozzle (optional)
Opal sparkle sugar (optional)

Speciality Tools
Two 20-cm cake tins

Continued on page 104

103

Continued from page 103

1. **To make the cake batter:** Line the bottom of both cake tins with rounds of parchment paper. Preheat the oven to 160°C Fan/180C/Gas 4.
2. Whisk the eggs in a medium bowl. Add the milk, orange zest, orange juice and vanilla and whisk to combine. Set aside.
3. In the bowl of a stand mixer fitted with the paddle attachment (or in a large mixing bowl using a hand mixer), combine the flour, sugar, baking powder and salt. Stir until combined. Add the softened butter, stirring on low until a coarse crumb mixture forms.
4. Reserve half of the egg mixture and add the rest to the batter mixture. Mix on medium (or high if using a hand mixer) for about 2 minutes. Stop the mixer. Add the remaining egg mixture and beat for 1 minute more. Stop the mixer again, scrape down the sides of the bowl and mix about 30 seconds more. Split the batter between the cake tins and bake for 20–25 minutes or until a cake skewer inserted in the centre comes out clean. Leave to cool in the tin for 15 minutes, then use an offset spatula to loosen the edge and invert onto a wire cooling rack.
5. **To make the truffles:** Place the chocolate in a microwave-safe bowl and pour the whipping cream over it. Heat in the microwave for 1 minute, leave to stand for 5 minutes and stir until smooth. Stir in the orange extract and ginger. Cover and refrigerate for 2–3 hours or until firm enough to work with.
6. Have a baking tray lined with a silicone mat or parchment ready. Remove the chocolate mixture from the fridge. Dust your hands with a bit of cornflour and make four large balls, 2 tablespoons each, by rolling the mixture in your hands. Make an additional four small balls, about 2 teaspoons each. Leave the truffles on the tray while you melt the coating.
7. Melt the coating of choice (see note) in a microwave-safe bowl, then stir until smooth.
8. Dip each ball into the coating, shake off the excess and return it to the baking tray. Save any extra coating to attach your chosen décor.
9. When all the truffles have been coated, place the baking tray in the fridge for 5 minutes to set. To make the snowman, use a bit of coating to glue one large and one small truffle together.
10. Decorate with a gummy sweet hat, liquorice scarf and hundreds and thousand eyes and buttons, using more coating to attach. Store the snowman and the remaining truffles in an airtight container, in the fridge until serving.
11. **To make the frosting:** In a microwave-safe bowl, melt the chocolate in 30-second bursts, stirring between each one. Stir until completely smooth.
12. In the bowl of a stand mixer fitted with a paddle attachment, beat the cream cheese for 2 minutes until smooth and fluffy. Scrape down the sides of the bowl. Add the chocolate in three batches, beating on low for 30 seconds and then high for 30 seconds more after each addition. Once all the chocolate is added, scrape down the bowl again. With the mixer running on medium-low, begin adding the butter, 1 tablespoon at a time, until it is all incorporated. Scrape the bowl again, switch to a whisk attachment, and add the orange juice and vanilla. Whip on high for about 30–60 seconds until light and fluffy.
13. Mix about 140g of the frosting with the marmalade and set aside.
14. **To assemble the cake:** Smear a bit of frosting on a cake plate or cake board and place the bottom layer on it. Frost the top of the bottom layer with the marmalade frosting mixture, spreading it evenly out to the sides. Top this with the second layer and use the remaining frosting to frost the entire cake, top and sides. To add the trees, fit a piping bag with a large open star nozzle and fill with the remaining frosting. Wherever you want a tree, pipe a large 'star' mound to create the base. Insert a pretzel stick into the centre of this base and insert the star nozzle over it, pushing gently to the base of the pretzel stick. Continue to pipe stars as you move the bag up the stick. Make sure to use less pressure with each star, creating smaller ones as you go. Chill until an hour before serving.
15. When you remove the cake from the fridge, you can decorate with the snowman and extra 'snowballs'. Use the sparkle sugar to create the snowman's skate lines.

Note | White chocolate is off-white. For a snowier look coat the truffles with the white candy melt coating.

Sleepy CUPCAKES

Makes: 24 cupcakes
Dietary Notes: V

Cakes & Tarts

During the Christmas holiday in *Harry Potter and the Chamber of Secrets*, Harry, Ron and Hermione endeavour to find the Heir of Slytherin, a descendant of Salazar Slytherin who has released the murderous Basilisk within the Chamber of Secrets to attack Muggle-born students. To do so, Hermione brews Polyjuice Potion so Harry and Ron can enter the Slytherin dormitory disguised as Draco Malfoy's cronies, Crabbe and Goyle. Their task is almost too easy as the Slytherins grab two floating cupcakes filled with a sleeping draught. These fluffy cupcakes will seem light enough to float themselves, with their tangy orange flavour and chocolate ganache topping.

> 'I've filled these with a simple sleeping draught. Simple but powerful.'
>
> —Hermione Granger,
> *Harry Potter and the Chamber of Secrets*

INGREDIENTS

For the Cake
3 eggs
240ml full-fat milk
1 tablespoon vanilla extract
Zest from 1 orange
1 tablespoon orange juice
300g plain flour
250g caster sugar
4 teaspoons baking powder
½ teaspoon kosher salt
170g unsalted butter, softened

For the Ganache
160g milk chocolate chips
240ml double cream
2 tablespoons orange sprinkles

Speciality Tools
Two 12-hole muffin tins

1. **To make the cake:** Preheat oven to 160°C Fan/180°C/Gas 4. Line the two muffin tins with paper cases.
2. Whisk the eggs in a medium bowl. Add the milk, vanilla, orange juice and zest. Whisk until combined and set aside.
3. In the bowl of a stand mixer fitted with the paddle attachment (or in a large mixing bowl using a hand mixer), combine the flour, sugar, baking powder and salt. Mix until combined. Add the softened butter, stirring on low until a coarse crumb mixture forms.
4. Reserving half of the milk mixture, add the rest to the flour mixture. Mix on medium (or high if using a hand mixer) for about 2 minutes. Stop the mixer, add the remaining milk, and beat for 1 minute more.
5. Stop the mixer again, scrape down the sides of the bowl and mix for about 30 seconds more. Fill each muffin case half full. Bake for 15—20 minutes or until a skewer inserted in the centre of the cake comes out clean. Leave the cupcakes to cool in the tin on a wire rack before removing. Leave to cool completely before frosting.
6. **To make the ganache:** Add the chocolate chips to a medium microwave-safe bowl and pour the cream over them. Heat in the microwave for 1 minute and then leave to stand for 5 minutes. Stir until smooth. Leave to cool for 10 minutes or until spreadable.
7. Spread a dollop of ganache onto the centre of each cupcake and top with sprinkles.
8. Cupcakes can be stored in a cool place in an airtight container for up to 3 days.

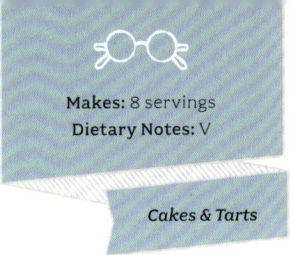

Makes: 8 servings
Dietary Notes: V

Cakes & Tarts

WIZARD CHESS PIE

While endeavouring to find the Philosopher's Stone, Harry, Ron and Hermione must pass through a series of security obstacles including a three-headed dog, flying keys and a deadly game of wizard chess. Ron is a talented player of the game and guides his friends to a win that allows Harry to continue on to locate the stone. The 'marble' of the chessboard's squares was created by squirting oil paint into a 2-metre square tank of water and then placing paper on top to absorb the swirling colours. This pie needs only a few drops of food colouring to create the board's black squares.

> 'That's wizard chess!'
>
> —Ron Weasley,
> *Harry Potter and the Philosopher's Stone*

INGREDIENTS

For the Pastry
340g plain flour
2 tablespoons caster sugar
1 teaspoon salt
2 teaspoons ground cinnamon
115g unsalted butter, very cold
60g solid vegetable shortening, very cold
80ml ice water
1 egg white, for egg wash
2–3 drops of black food colouring

For the Filling
1 egg
4 egg yolks
130g granulated sugar
130g dark brown sugar
¼ teaspoon salt
80ml double cream
80ml full-fat milk
6 tablespoons salted butter, cut into small chunks

For the Topping
140g walnuts
Cinnamon sugar, from above
1 teaspoon vegetable oil

Continued on page 108

Continued from page 107

1. **To make the pastry:** In a large bowl, combine the flour, salt, 1 tablespoon of the sugar and ½ teaspoon of the cinnamon. Cut the butter and shortening into tablespoon-size pieces and add to the flour mixture. Use a pastry cutter or two forks to cut into the flour. Add the water a little bit at a time and mix gently until the dough comes together.

2. On a lightly floured surface, roll out half the pastry to line a 23-cm tin. Trim the pastry with a sharp knife to a 1-cm overhang around the edge. Fold the overhang under and crimp the edges with your fingers.

3. Roll out the other half of the dough and cut out squares 2.5 by 2.5cm using a cookie cutter or sharp knife. Cut out at least 25 squares and place them on a baking tray lined with a silicone baking mat or parchment paper. Chill both the pastry shell and the squares for 30 minutes.

4. Towards the end of the chill time, preheat the oven to 200°C Fan/220°C/Gas 7 and prepare an egg wash by mixing the egg with 1 tablespoon water and a few drops of black food colouring in a small bowl. In a separate small bowl, mix the remaining 1 tablespoon sugar and the remaining 1½ teaspoons cinnamon.

5. When the pastry is done chilling, brush the squares with the egg wash and sprinkle with about half of the cinnamon sugar, reserving the remaining cinnamon sugar for the topping. Line the pastry with foil and baking beans or dried beans and bake both the pastry and squares for 10 minutes. Remove the tart tin from the oven, remove the foil and weights and brush the bottom of the pastry with the egg wash. Brush every other crimped edge with the egg wash. Return to the oven for another 7—10 minutes. Keep an eye on the squares and remove them from the oven when they are crisp and starting to brown. Remove the pastry from the oven and leave to cool. When both the pastry and squares are baked, lower the oven temperature to 115°C Fan/135°C/Gas 1 and have the rack in the centre of the oven.

6. **To make the filling:** In a medium heatproof bowl, whisk together the egg, egg yolks, granulated sugar, brown sugar and salt until well combined. Whisk in the cream and milk. In a large frying pan over medium-high heat, bring 2.5cm of water to the boil. Turn the heat down to medium and place the bowl into the water. Scatter the butter pieces over the filling mixture and whisk until the butter is melted and the mixture is shiny and warm to the touch.

7. Place the pastry in the centre of the oven rack and pour the filling into the crust. Bake for about 45—50 minutes or until the edges of the filling are set but the centre still has some jiggle when the tin is nudged. Remove from the oven and leave to cool completely on a wire rack. The pie should be stored in the fridge and can be kept for up to 3 days. Leave to come to room temperature before serving and place the baked squares on top of the pie just before serving.

8. **To make the nut topping:** In a small frying pan over high heat, add the walnuts and toast for 1 minute. Turn the heat down to medium. Add the remaining cinnamon sugar and the vegetable oil. Stir to combine. Continue toasting until the sugar starts to liquify, stirring constantly. Remove to a plate to cool. Serve alongside the chess pie and add a bit to each bite.

Butterscotch ICE CREAM PIE

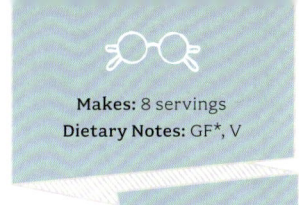

Makes: 8 servings
Dietary Notes: GF*, V

Cakes & Tarts

With butterscotch ice cream, whipped cream and butterscotch sweets, this pie might make Hermione Granger's dentist parents shudder, but the taste is magical. Inspired by the most popular wizarding drink — Butterbeer — the pie starts with a shortbread biscuit crust and ends with mouthwatering delight. Butterbeer is everywhere in the wizarding world; graphic designers Miraphora Mina and Eduardo Lima have created bottle labels for the brand for Harry Potter's time in the 1990s, and for 1920s Britain and 1930s Bhutan, seen in the Fantastic Beasts films. This recipe uses the Butterscotch Ice Cream seen on page 127 and the recipe for Shortbread Christmas Biscuits dough on page 118.

> 'Does anyone fancy a Butterbeer?'
>
> —Harry Potter,
> *Harry Potter and the Half-Blood Prince*

INGREDIENTS

150g shortbread biscuit crumbs, from Shortbread Christmas Biscuits (see page 118)

4 tablespoons salted butter, melted

2 tablespoons caster sugar

80g fudge pieces

1 recipe Butterscotch Ice Cream (see page 127), or 1-litre shop-bought ice cream

120ml double cream

Speciality Tools
Whipped cream canister (see note)

1. In the base of a 23-cm pie plate, mix together the biscuit crumbs, melted butter and sugar until well blended. Use your hands or another pie plate to press the crumb mixture in an even layer on the bottom and up the sides of the pie plate. Freeze for at least 1 hour.

2. While the crust is freezing, let the ice cream soften in the fridge.

3. Spread half of the ice cream into the bottom of the biscuit crust, sprinkle with half the fudge pieces and top with the remaining ice cream. Cover in cling film and freeze for at least 2 hours or up to 2 days.

4. Reserve the remaining fudge pieces in an airtight container until ready to serve.

5. About 30 minutes before serving, fill a whipped cream canister with the double cream. Remove the pie from the freezer, decorate the top with whipped cream rosettes, sprinkle each rosette with the remaining fudge pieces and refrigerate the pie until serving.

6. If the crust is sticking to the pie plate, place the bottom of the pie plate in warm water for about 30 seconds.

Note | If you don't have a whipped cream canister, whip the cream in a large bowl with a hand mixer until stiff peaks form. Load the whipped cream into a piping bag fitted with a large star nozzle or use a large spoon to make dollops instead of rosettes.

Makes: 12 Servings
Dietary Notes: V

Cakes & Tarts

Great Hall
FLOATING CANDLE CAKE

The Great Hall at Hogwarts is filled with light — a blazing fireplace, glowing flambeaux and candles that float above the room, illuminating every feast and fête. The floating candles were initially produced by suspending real lights from wires, but it was quickly realized they would be better created digitally. This then allowed the computer artists to assign unique flame cycles, vary the models and float them in arrangements that included spirals, arches, tiers and star shapes. This chocolate cake, with a chocolate ganache filling and brown butter frosting, 'burns' by a flaked almond wick to light up your dessert table.

> 'Welcome to Hogwarts. Now, in a few moments, you will pass through these doors and join your classmates.'
>
> —Minerva McGonagall,
> *Harry Potter and the Philosopher's Stone*

INGREDIENTS

For the Cake
225g unsalted butter
300g light brown sugar
300g granulated sugar
4 eggs
1 tablespoon vanilla extract
200g cocoa powder
400g plain flour
4 teaspoons baking powder
½ teaspoon salt
285g sour cream
480ml hot coffee

For the Filling
200g chopped pecans
2 teaspoons vegetable oil
2 tablespoons sugar

For the Frosting
6 egg whites
¼ teaspoon salt
400g dark brown sugar
1 teaspoon fresh lemon juice
675g unsalted butter, cut into tablespoons, plus more for greasing
2 teaspoons vanilla extract
160g milk chocolate chips

For Assembly
3 wooden skewers
1 blanched almond

Speciality Tools
Three 15-cm cake tins
2 piping bags
1 large writing nozzle (about #8)
1 medium writing nozzle (about #4)

Continued on page 112

Continued from page 111

1. **To make the cake:** Preheat the oven to 160°C Fan/180°C/Gas 4. Line three 15-cm cake tins with rounds of parchment paper fitted in the bottom.
2. In the bowl of a stand mixer fitted with the paddle attachment, cream together the butter, brown sugar and granulated sugar on medium-high speed for about 3 minutes until light and fluffy. Add the eggs and vanilla. Beat again until well combined. Add the cocoa powder and mix again until completely incorporated.
3. In a small bowl, mix together the flour, baking powder and salt.
4. Add half of the flour mixture to the butter mixture and mix until incorporated. Scrape down the sides of the bowl and add the sour cream all at once. Mix until incorporated. Add the remaining flour mixture, mix again and scrape down the sides of the bowl.
5. With the mixer running on low speed, slowly drizzle in the hot coffee. Continue to mix for 2–3 minutes until all of the coffee is incorporated and batter is smooth.
6. Split the batter evenly between the prepared cake tins and bake for 25–30 minutes, or until a skewer inserted into the centre of the cake comes out clean. Leave to cool in the tins for 15 minutes before inverting onto a wire rack and removing the parchment. Leave to cool completely.
7. Cut the dome tops off of two of the three cakes, and cut each cake into two even layers. Discard the cake scraps or reserve for future use. Place the layers in an airtight container between layers of parchment and freeze while you make the filling and frosting.
8. **To make the filling:** Heat a medium frying pan over medium-high heat for 1 minute, add the pecans and toast, stirring continuously, for 1 minute more. Turn the heat down to medium-low and add the oil and sugar. Continue stirring until most of the sugar dissolves. Transfer the pecans to a plate and allow to cool completely.
9. **To make the frosting:** Add the egg whites and salt to the bowl of a stand mixer fitted with a whisk attachment. In a medium heavy-bottomed saucepan over medium-high heat, combine the brown sugar with 240ml water and bring to the boil. Set the mixer on medium speed and whisk the egg whites for about 1 minute until frothy. Add the lemon juice and whisk for 2–3 minutes more until soft peaks form, then shut off the mixer.
10. Grease a heatproof 1-litre measuring jug with butter and set aside. Fit the saucepan with a sugar thermometer and, when the sugar mixture reaches 114°C, decant it to the measuring jug.
11. Slowly add the sugar syrup to the egg whites in small batches, whisking after each addition. When all the syrup is added, beat the mixture on high speed for 3–5 minutes until the meringue is completely cool (the outside of the bowl should be cool to the touch).

12. Add the butter, one to two pieces at a time, beating well on medium speed after each addition. Once all the butter has been incorporated, add the vanilla and briefly beat on high speed until smooth.

13. In a medium microwave-safe bowl, add the chocolate chips. Heat for 1 minute and then leave to stand for 5 minutes. Stir until smooth, allow to cool for 1–2 minutes and then stir into about 350g of the buttercream.

14. **To assemble the cake:** On a cake stand or small cake board, spread a bit of the chocolate buttercream and place the first layer on top. Put 70g of the chocolate buttercream over the top of this first layer and smooth out with an offset spatula. Sprinkle with some of the pecan filling. Repeat these steps with the next four layers, then top with the sixth layer. Use any remaining chocolate frosting to seal the edges of the layers. Press three skewers, evenly placed, through the top layer all the way to the bottom, trimming off any excess skewer. This will ensure that this extra tall cake stays stable. Refrigerate for 30 minutes.

15. Remove the cake from the fridge and use an offset spatula to frost the top and sides of the cake with the buttercream. Smooth the sides, and create a low point in the middle of the top by pushing frosting towards the edges. Place about 130g of the frosting in a piping bag fitted with a large writing nozzle and pipe the 'melted' rim of the candle. Use the offset spatula to smooth and sculpt this, disguising the piping and creating a wax look. Chill the cake for another 30 minutes.

16. Gently heat about 130g of the frosting in the microwave for 5–10 seconds only. Load this frosting into a piping bag fitted with the medium writing nozzle. Remove the cake from the fridge and use the frosting to create the 'wax drips'. The cold cake will stop the drips as they slide down making the candle effect.

17. Refrigerate until an hour before serving, then remove and leave to come to room temperature. Place the blanched almond as the wick in the centre of the cake. The almond will light briefly if desired. The best way to cut this extra tall cake is to cut halfway down from the top, and then cut in from the side, removing slices that are three layers tall. Once the top has been served the bottom three layers can be cut as usual.

Makes: About 30 Pops
Dietary Notes: V

Biscuits

'I'm Sorry, Neville'
BISCUIT POPS

By using the Marauder's Map and his Invisibility Cloak in *Harry Potter and the Prisoner of Azkaban*, Harry makes his way into Honeydukes sweet shop in Hogsmeade and steals a large red lollipop from Neville Longbottom on his way through the shop. This version is a chocolate cookie made with a peppermint sweet centre that gives the shiny appearance of stained glass. Because it was a bit unfair of Harry to lift Neville's sweet, 'I'm Sorry, Neville' is piped around the edge in frosting in hopes of forgiveness.

> **'Why is it always me?'**
> —Neville Longbottom,
> *Harry Potter and the Chamber of Secrets*

Continued on page 116

Continued from page 115

INGREDIENTS

6 tablespoons salted butter, softened

55g cream cheese, softened

100g caster sugar

25g dark cocoa powder

1 egg

½ teaspoon peppermint extract

200g plain flour

About 30 unwrapped peppermint sweets

About 30 lollipop sticks (optional)

About 130g white Royal Icing from Golden Trio Biscuits (see page 122)

Speciality Tools

7.5- and 2.5-cm fluted round cookie cutters

Piping bags and writing nozzles

1. Line two baking trays with a silicone baking mat or parchment paper.

2. In the bowl of a stand mixer fitted with a paddle attachment, beat the butter, cream cheese and sugar together for about 3 minutes until light and fluffy. Scrape down the sides of the bowl, add the cocoa and mix again until well combined. Add the egg and peppermint extract and mix again.

3. Slowly add the flour, 60g at a time, mixing on low each time, until well combined. Form the dough into a disk, wrap it in parchment paper and refrigerate for at least 1 hour.

4. On a lightly floured surface, roll out the dough to about 3mm thick and cut out as many 7.5-cm circles as possible. Transfer the circles to the baking tray, spacing out so there is enough room for the lollipop sticks, if using. Reroll the scraps and cut out more 7.5-cm circles. Use the 2.5-cm cutter to cut the centre out of all the large circles. You can either reroll the small circles to make more lollipops or bake them as tiny bonus biscuits.

5. Place a peppermint sweet in the centre of each biscuit. Gently lift the bottom of each biscuit and place a lollipop stick under the dough, just to the edge of the central hole. Gently press the dough against the stick.

6. Chill the biscuits in the fridge for 10 minutes. While the biscuits are chilling, preheat the oven to 160°C Fan/180°C/Gas 4. Bake for 9—11 minutes or until the biscuits are firm and the sweet has melted to fill the centre.

7. Leave to cool completely on the baking tray. Once cool they can be stored in an airtight container between layers of parchment paper for up to 5 days or wrapped in cellophane bags as favours.

8. If decorating, put the Royal icing in a piping bag fitted with a writing nozzle and write, 'I'm sorry, Neville!' around the sweet centre. Leave the icing to dry for at least 1 hour before packaging or storing. The mini cente biscuits can be decorated as snowflakes.

Common Room
JAM SANDWICH BISCUITS

Makes: About 24 sandwich biscuits and 24 mini biscuits
Dietary Notes: V

Biscuits

In the common room for Harry's first Christmas is a small evergreen tree in a pot set next to the crackling fireplace, decorated, not surprisingly, in the house colours, with miniature gold Christmas crackers, lanterns and presents wrapped in red paper hanging from its branches. The Slytherin common room is bereft of holiday décor, but if it had any, it would be done in silver and green. These 'windowed' sugar cookies, which use the Golden Trio Biscuits dough seen on page 122, can be decorated in any house's colours, like yellow and black for Hufflepuff or blue and silver for Ravenclaw. Of course, using red and green sorts you into Christmas!

> 'Welcome to the Gryffindor common room. Boys' dormitory is upstairs and down to your left. Girls' the same on your right.'
>
> —Percy Weasley,
> *Harry Potter and the Philosopher's Stone*

Note | Perform a quick set test. Before you start to cook the jam, place a small plate in the freezer. After cooking the jam for at least 15 minutes, remove the plate from the freezer and put about 1 tablespoon of jam on it. When the plate is tilted, the jam should move only slowly, or barely at all. If it still runs quickly, pop the plate back into the freezer, continue to cook the jam for another 5 minutes and check again.

INGREDIENTS

For the Sandwich Biscuits
1 recipe Golden Trio Biscuits dough, chilled (see page 122)

About 50g sanding sugar, in various colours

1 jar homemade jam, see below, or shop-bought jam

For the Jam
150g crushed raspberries

600g granulated sugar

Juice of 1 lemon

Speciality Tools
4 clean 225-ml jam jars with tight-fitting lids

Fluted cookie cutters, in various shapes, in 7.5-cm and 4-cm sizes

1. **To make the biscuits:** Preheat the oven to 170°C Fan/190°C/Gas 5. Line two baking trays with silicone baking mats or parchment paper.

2. On a lightly floured surface and working with one disk of biscuit dough at a time, roll out the dough to 3mm thick. Cut out pairs of 7.5-cm shapes and use their coordinating small shapes to cut a window from one biscuit of each pair. Use the edge of an offset spatula or the point of a knife to remove the small shape from the centre and place it on the baking tray. Sprinkle the windowed half and the small biscuit with sanding sugar, pressing it gently into the dough.

3. Repeat until you have cut out as many sets as you can. Chill in the fridge for at least 10 minutes before baking for about 9–11 minutes. Repeat with the second disk.

4. **To make the jam:** Run the raspberries through a food mill or press through a sieve to remove about half the seeds.

5. Add the fruit to a large saucepan and combine it with the sugar and the lemon juice. Bring to a rolling boil over high heat. Reduce to medium heat, stirring frequently, and keep at a low boil for 15–20 minutes or until a quick set test shows gelling (see note).

6. Remove the mixture from the heat, ladle into four clean jars and seal with tight-fitting lids. Leave the jam to cool for about 30 minutes and then refrigerate until serving. The jam can be stored in the refrigerator for 1 month or in the freezer for 6 months. Jam makes a great gift; just be sure to label it appropriately: 'Keep refrigerated for up to 1 month.'

7. To serve, spread a thin layer of jam, about ½ teaspoon, onto the biscuit base and top with its matching window. Serve right away or store in an airtight container, between layers of parchment paper, for up to 5 days.

Makes: About 32 5-cm by 2.5-cm bars
Dietary Notes: V

Biscuits

Shortbread
CHRISTMAS BISCUITS

Shortbread is a traditional Scottish biscuit, seen everywhere around the country during the Christmas holidays. Nicknamed a 'shortie', and known to be a favourite of Mary, Queen of Scots, these biscuits are a crisp and crumbly indulgence. It is never specifically mentioned in the books that Hogwarts is in Scotland, but production designer Stuart Craig decided that was where they should look for the backgrounds to the films, with its sparkling lochs and rugged mountains.

> 'I hope there's pudding.'
>
> —Luna Lovegood,
> *Harry Potter and the Order of the Phoenix*

INGREDIENTS

140g unsalted butter

½ teaspoon sea salt

35g icing sugar

1½ tablespoons granulated sugar

200g plain flour

Speciality Tools
20-by-20-cm baking tin

1. Prepare a bowl with an ice bath that a heatproof measuring jug will fit into. Line the baking tin with 2 strips of parchment paper that overhang the edges.
2. Add the butter to a small saucepan over medium-low heat and stir gently until the butter is melted. Continue cooking, stirring occasionally, for 15–20 minutes until the butter separates, turns a deep amber and smells very nutty. Transfer the butter to a heatproof measuring jug and place it in the ice bath. Leave the butter to cool, stirring occasionally, for 20 minutes until it is the consistency of softened butter.
3. Preheat the oven to 130°C Fan/150°C/Gas 2.
4. Transfer the brown butter to a medium bowl and add the salt, icing sugar and 1 tablespoon of the granulated sugar. Beat on medium speed for 1–2 minutes with a hand mixer until light and fluffy.
5. Sift the flour over the butter mixture, a little at a time, folding it in between each addition. When all the flour has been incorporated, press the mixture into an even layer in the baking tin. Use a fork to prick the dough all over the surface.
6. Bake for 40–45 minutes or until a pale golden brown with slightly darker edges. Leave to cool until warm to the touch and score with a sharp knife into bars. Sprinkle with the remaining ½ tablespoon granulated sugar and leave to cool completely.
7. When completely cool, use the parchment to lift from the tin and use the score lines to cut through completely. Store in an airtight container for up to 1 week.

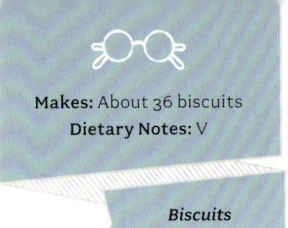

Makes: About 36 biscuits
Dietary Notes: V

Biscuits

Golden Trio
BISCUITS

The 'Golden Trio' of bespectacled Harry Potter, bushy-haired Hermione Granger and ginger Ron Weasley are familiar faces to any Harry Potter fan, and like their characters, the three actors in their parts got along very well. Daniel Radcliffe (Harry Potter) attributes this to the fact that they were like Harry, Hermione and Ron. He described Rupert Grint (Ron Weasley) as funny, Emma Watson (Hermione Granger) as very intelligent, and himself as being 'in between', because that's how he thought of Harry. These Golden Trio Biscuits pay a sweet tribute to the undaunted heroes and fast friends.

> 'Holy Cricket! You're Harry Potter. I'm Hermione Granger. And you are?'
>
> 'I'm Ron Weasley.'
>
> 'Pleasure.'
>
> —Hermione Granger and Ron Weasley, *Harry Potter and the Philosopher's Stone*

Continued on page 122

Continued from page 121

INGREDIENTS

For the Dough
170g salted butter, softened
125g cream cheese, softened
150g light brown sugar
1 egg
1 teaspoon vanilla extract
400g plain flour
6-cm to 7.5-cm cookie cutter

For the Royal Icing
565g icing sugar, sifted
3 tablespoons meringue powder
1—2 drops each black, green, blue, brown and orange food colouring

Speciality Tools
Piping bags and writing nozzles

1. **To make the dough:** In a large bowl, beat together the butter, cream cheese and sugar until light and fluffy. Add the egg and vanilla and beat again until well combined. Add the flour, a little at a time, mixing on low and mixing by hand with the last part.

2. Split the dough in half, form into disks, wrap in parchment paper and chill for at least 1 hour. Towards the end of the hour, preheat the oven to 170°C Fan/190°C/Gas 5.

3. After chilling the dough, work with one half at a time on a lightly floured surface. Roll out each disk to 3mm thick and cut out as many circles as you can with the cookie cutter. Transfer the rounds to a baking tray, rewrap the scraps and chill both the scraps and the rounds while working with the second disk.

4. Repeat with the second disk and make sure the rounds chill for at least 10 minutes before baking. Bake for 9—11 minutes or until just starting to brown at the edges. Leave to cool on a wire rack.

5. **To make the Royal icing:** In the bowl of a stand mixer fitted with the whisk attachment, combine the icing sugar, meringue powder and 6 tablespoons water. Whisk on low speed for 7—10 minutes, or until the icing holds stiff peaks. (If using a hand mixer, whisk on high speed for 10—12 minutes.)

6. Divide the icing into 5 small bowls and use the food colouring to create your desired colours. Transfer the icing to piping bags fitted with writing nozzles.

7. To decorate, create each character's face on a biscuit round, starting by creating their hair across the top quarter of the biscuit and going from there. Have fun! See how many other designs you can create with just a round: Hedwig's face, Trevor the toad, a Remembrall?

8. Leave the biscuits to dry completely for at least 3 hours before serving, packaging or storing. Store in an airtight container between layers of parchment paper or place each biscuit in a cellophane bag for gifting.

Professor Trelawney's
POTS DE CRÈME

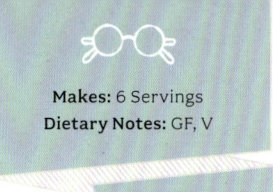

Makes: 6 Servings
Dietary Notes: GF, V

Special Puddings

Pot de Crème became popular in the 17th century as a creamy sweet that was baked in a porcelain cup. This tea-infused version was inspired by the myriad tea cups seen in Professor Trelawney's Divination classroom, used for the art of Tessomancy. Tessomancy predicts the future through the reading of tea leaves (although Trelawney always seems to see something negative!). There were more than 500 tea cups in her room, many of these stacked on a table forming a towering china pyramid.

> 'Look in the cup — tell me what you see!'
> —Sybill Trelawney, Harry Potter and the Prisoner of Azkaban

Note | Choose tea cups without any metallic leaf décor because they can be delicate and might be damaged by the water bath.

INGREDIENTS

- 100g caster sugar
- 6 egg yolks
- 360ml full-fat milk
- 120ml lower fat cream
- 1 teaspoon vanilla extract
- 2 teaspoons brandy (optional)
- 3 English breakfast tea bags (or 1 tablespoon loose leaf tea)

Speciality Tools
Six 120-ml ramekins or tea cups (see note)
Glass baking dish large enough to fit all six ramekins or tea cups, lined with a clean tea towel

1. Preheat the oven to 170°C Fan/190°C/Gas 5.
2. In a medium bowl, whisk together the sugar and egg yolks until well combined and pale in colour.
3. In a small saucepan over medium heat, combine the milk and cream with the vanilla and brandy, if using. Open the tea bags and stir the contents into the milk mixture. Stirring continuously, heat the milk until it comes to a simmer.
4. Remove from the heat and gradually whisk the milk into the egg mixture about 60ml at a time. When all the milk has been incorporated, strain the mixture through a fine-mesh sieve into a heatproof measuring jug. Skim any foam off the top with a small spoon.
5. Split the custard evenly between the six containers and top each container with a tight-fitting piece of foil. Place each container in the baking dish on top of the tea towel. Place the baking dish in the oven and fill with scalding water until the level reaches halfway up the sides of the containers. Bake for 45–50 minutes or until set but with a bit of jiggle in the centre.
6. Using a dry tea towel or tongs, carefully remove the custards from the water bath to a cooling rack and leave them to cool for 30 minutes. After 30 minutes, refrigerate for at least 2 hours before serving. These can be made up to 3 days ahead and kept, covered in the refrigerator.

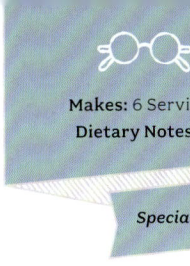

Makes: 6 Servings
Dietary Notes: V

Special Puddings

Hogsmeade
INVISIBLE SNOWBALLS

To make Harry's trip to Hogsmeade possible in *Harry Potter and the Prisoner of Azkaban*, he utilizes his Invisibility Cloak so he will not be seen. Then, when Hermione and Ron are bullied by Draco and his friends, Harry, under the cloak, peppers them with snowballs that seem to come out of thin air, frightening the Slytherin trio so much they run away. The Invisibility Cloak used by Daniel Radcliffe was constructed with green-screen material on one side that he would flip over himself to disappear or reappear. These white chocolate snowballs hide a Blondie that appears when a hot chocolate sauce is poured over the shell.

> 'Who's there?'
>
> —Draco Malfoy,
> *Harry Potter and the Prisoner of Azkaban*

Continued on page 126

Continued from page 125

INGREDIENTS

For the Brownies
55g white chocolate
85g salted butter
50g light brown sugar
½ teaspoon vanilla extract
2 eggs
65g plain flour
240g dark chocolate chips

For the Snowballs
180g white chocolate
White lustre dust (optional)

For the Ganache
300ml whipping cream
¼ teaspoon ground cinnamon
⅛ teaspoon cayenne pepper

Speciality Tools
six 7.5-cm silicone sphere moulds

1. **To make the brownie:** Preheat the oven to 160°C Fan/180°C/Gas 4 and prepare 7.5-cm silicone sphere moulds by placing them on a baking tray.

2. In a microwave-safe bowl, add the white chocolate and the butter. Microwave for 1 minute and then stir until the butter and chocolate are completely melted. Add the sugar and stir until well combined. Add the vanilla and eggs and stir vigorously until well combined. Add the flour and stir again. Fold in 80g of the dark chocolate chips.

3. Split the batter between the six sphere mould cavities. Bake for 15—20 minutes or until golden around the edges and a skewer comes out with just a few crumbs when inserted in the centre of the cake. Cool for 10 minutes in the moulds, then unmould and leave to cool completely on a wire rack.

4. **To make the snowballs:** Melt the white chocolate in a double boiler or microwave-safe bowl until just melted. Using the same moulds (well cleaned and dried) and a pastry brush, dust six cavities with lustre dust if using. Using the same brush, coat the cavities with a thin layer of chocolate. Make sure there are no blank spots, and go all the way to the edges. Place the moulds in the fridge for 10 minutes to set.

5. **To make the ganache:** In a microwave-safe bowl, combine the cream with the remaining chocolate chips. Heat the mixture for 1 minute and then leave to stand for 5 minutes. After 5 minutes, stir until smooth, add the cinnamon and cayenne and stir again. Set aside.

6. **To assemble:** Carefully remove the chocolate shells from the moulds. Line a baking tray with parchment paper. Heat a small plate in the microwave for 30 seconds and clean up the rims of each shell by twisting the edge against the warm plate, then place on parchment to cool.

7. When ready to serve, place each brownie on a small dessert plate and cover with a chocolate shell. Reheat the ganache for 1—1½ minutes in the microwave until it is quite warm, and give each guest a small jug or glass of it on the side. Each person can pour ganache over the top to melt the 'snowball'.

Makes: 1 litre
Dietary Notes: GF, V

Special Puddings

Butterscotch ICE CREAM

A tribute to Butterbeer, this no-churn butterscotch ice cream will definitely hit your sweet spot. Ice cream is a common wizarding treat: eighty towers of No-Melt ice cream were created for the Triwizard Tournament's welcoming feast, which was made up of only puddings and desserts. The No-Melt ice cream was completely inedible, made from a combination of resin and tiny glass beads that gave it a magical iridescence as well as a credible-looking ice cream texture. This butterscotch confection is unlike the wizarding world's non-melting version, but once tasted, it probably won't last long enough to melt anyway.

> 'Three Butterbeers and some ginger and lime, please.'
>
> —Hermione Granger,
> *Harry Potter and the Half-Blood Prince*

INGREDIENTS

One 400-g tin sweetened condensed milk

100g dark brown sugar

1 tablespoon Scotch whiskey, or whiskey extract

2 teaspoons vanilla extract

600ml whipping cream

1. In a medium saucepan over medium heat, combine the sweetened condensed milk, brown sugar whiskey and vanilla. Stir and bring to the boil. Continue boiling, stirring almost continuously for 5–8 minutes or until the mixture darkens and thickens considerably.

2. Remove from heat and transfer the mixture to the bowl of a stand mixer fitted with a whisk attachment. Whisk on medium-high until the sides of the bowl are completely cool. This could take up to 15 minutes. Be careful not to let your mixer overheat.

3. Stop the mixer and add the cream one-third at a time, mixing on low until incorporated with the butterscotch mixture. Once all the cream has been combined, increase the speed to high and mix until stiff peaks form. Stop frequently to scrape down the sides of the bowl. Transfer the mixture to an airtight container and freeze for a minimum of 6 hours or overnight.

Makes: 6 servings
Dietary Notes: V

Special Puddings

Professor Flitwick's
CHRISTMAS FIGGY PUDDING

Figgy Pudding is a steamed cake, rather than the custardy, creamy pudding dessert as the name might suggest. Figgy Pudding is a staple of the Christmas holiday table and has been immortalized in song in the traditional Christmas carol 'We Wish You A Merry Christmas'. As Charms professor, Flitwick is the master of the *Wingardium Leviosa* spell and uses it to suspend Christmas ornaments onto the trees in the Great Hall in *Harry Potter and the Philosopher's Stone*. Mixing the fruit with a bit of flour helps keep it from sinking to the bottom, staying 'suspended' and evenly distributed, which illuminates the magic of baking.

INGREDIENTS

- 180g dried figs
- 200g plain flour
- 1 teaspoon baking powder
- 2 teaspoon ground cinnamon
- 2 teaspoons ground ginger
- ½ teaspoon allspice
- ½ teaspoon salt
- 65g dried currants
- 115g unsalted butter, plus more for greasing
- 200g dark brown sugar
- 3 eggs
- 2 teaspoons vanilla extract
- Whipped cream or ice cream, for serving (optional)

Speciality Tools
Six 180-ml ramekins

> 'Oh, well done! See here, everyone! Ms. Granger's done it! Oh, splendid!'
>
> —Filius Flitwick,
> *Harry Potter and the Philosopher's Stone*

1. Add the figs to a medium heatproof bowl and cover with 240ml boiling water. Leave for 15 minutes.
2. In a small bowl, mix together the flour, baking powder, cinnamon, ginger, allspice and salt. Set aside.
3. Drain the figs over a bowl, reserving both the fruit and the liquid. Cut six figs in half and roughly chop the remaining figs. Toss the chopped figs and the currants with 30g of the flour mixture. Set aside.
4. Preheat the oven to 170°C Fan/190°C/Gas 5 and grease the ramekins, setting them in a 23-by-32-cm casserole dish.
5. In the bowl of a stand mixer fitted with a paddle attachment, combine the butter and sugar together for about 2 minutes until light and fluffy. Add the eggs one at a time, mixing after each addition. Add the vanilla and mix again.
6. Add half of the remaining flour mixture and mix on low, then scrape down the sides of the bowl. Add the reserved fig liquid and mix again, ending with the remaining flour. Mix again until all the flour is incorporated. Remove the bowl from the stand mixer, scrape down the sides and fold in the fruit.
7. Place 2 fig halves, cut side facing the bottom, into each ramekin. These will be the top of your pudding if you serve it unmoulded. Split the batter between the ramekins, filling each about half full.
8. Place all the ramekins in the casserole dish, fill the pan with hot water until the water level is halfway up the ramekins and cover the whole dish with foil. Carefully place in the oven and bake for about 35–40 minutes or until set. Remove from the oven and transfer the ramekins to a wire rack. Serve warm in the ramekins or to unmould, run a knife around the edge of the pudding, cover with a plate and invert to unmould. Serve with whipped cream or ice cream, if desired.

Makes: 12 servings
Dietary Notes: V

Special Puddings

Triwizard TRIFLE

Trifle, a layered dessert of fruits, cake, custard and whipped cream, originated in 18th-century England according to tradition, so it has not been around as long as the 700-year-old Triwizard Tournament. This Trifle's components were inspired by the three schools that compete: Hogwarts (sponge cake), Beauxbatons (custard) and Durmstrang (lingonberry syrup). Hogwarts champions Cedric Diggory and Harry Potter grab the radiant Triwizard Cup together for the win. Inside the cup, a practical light gave it its glow. After sharing this Triwizard Trifle, your insides might glow as well.

> 'Eternal glory! That's what awaits the student who wins the Triwizard Tournament.'
>
> —Albus Dumbledore,
> *Harry Potter and the Goblet of Fire*

Continued on page 132

Continued from page 131

INGREDIENTS

For the Pastry Cream
100g caster sugar
3 tablespoons plain flour
3 tablespoons cornflour
6 egg yolks
480ml full-fat milk
¾ teaspoon almond extract
1½ teaspoons vanilla extract

For the Cake
3 eggs
240ml full-fat milk
1 tablespoon vanilla extract
300g plain flour
250g caster sugar
4 teaspoons baking powder
½ teaspoon kosher salt
175g unsalted butter, softened

For the Lingonberry Syrup
300g lingonberry sauce
240ml water
60ml orange liqueur or orange juice

For Assembly
360g fresh raspberries, rinsed and drained, plus a few more for garnish
2 tablespoons icing sugar
360ml whipping cream

Speciality Tools
Two 15-cm cake tins

1. **To make the pastry cream:** Add the sugar, flour, cornflour and egg yolks to a medium bowl. Use a hand mixer, fitted with the whisk attachment, to beat on high speed until thick and light in colour.

2. In a medium stainless steel saucepan, over medium-high heat, bring the milk to a simmer.

3. Remove the milk from the heat and pour about ⅓ of it into the egg mixture, stirring to combine. Transfer the milk/egg mixture back into the pan with the remaining milk and return to the stove, on medium-low heat. Whisk constantly, making sure to scrape the bottom and sides of the pan to prevent hot spots or burning. Just as the custard starts to thicken, add the almond and vanilla extracts. Continue to cook for another minute.

4. Remove from the heat and transfer into a clean bowl or airtight container. Press a piece of parchment paper against the surface of the custard to prevent a skin from forming. Leave to cool for 10—15 minutes. Leaving the parchment paper in place, cover the container with a lid or cling film and refrigerate for at least 1 hour or up to 2 days.

5. **To make the cake:** Grease and flour the bottom of two 15-cm cake tins, or cover with parchment paper cut to fit the bottoms. Preheat the oven to 170°C Fan/190°C/Gas 5.

6. Whisk the eggs in a medium bowl. Add the milk and vanilla and whisk to combine. Set aside.

7. In the bowl of a stand mixer fitted with the paddle attachment (or in a large mixing bowl using a hand mixer), combine the flour, sugar, baking powder and salt. Mix until combined. Add the softened butter, stirring on low until a coarse crumb mixture forms.

8. Reserve 120ml of the milk mixture and add the rest to the flour mixture. Mix on medium (or high if using a hand mixer) for about 2 minutes. Stop the mixer, add the remaining milk and beat for 1 minute more. Stop the mixer again, scrape down the sides of the bowl and mix about 30 seconds more. Pour batter into the prepared cake tins, splitting the batter evenly between the 2 tins.

9. Bake for 15–20 minutes or until a skewer inserted into the centre of the cake comes out clean. Remove cakes from the oven and leave to cool for 15 minutes in the tin. Run an offset spatula gently around the edges of the cake tins to loosen. Cover the cake tin with a baking tray or plate and flip over to release the cake from the tin. Transfer to a wire rack until completely cool.

10. Trim the domed top from each cake and then cut each cake into two layers. For the trifle you will only need three of the four layers. Reserve the tops and the fourth layer for another purpose such as Every Flavour Cake Pops (see page 91).

11. **To make the syrup:** Combine the lingonberry sauce, water and orange liqueur in a small saucepan over medium-high heat and bring to the boil. Turn the heat down to medium-low and simmer for 1 minute. Transfer to a heatproof bowl and refrigerate until cool. Once cool, the syrup can be used right away or stored in an airtight container for up to 5 days.

12. **To assemble:** Have a large trifle bowl or glass bowl standing by.

13. Make four straight slices across a cake layer and then three in the other direction, creating cubes. Lay the cake cubes in the bottom of the trifle bowl, recreating the circle, and make sure the pieces press up against the sides of the bowl.

14. Drizzle about one-quarter of the lingonberry syrup over the cake and use a pastry brush to spread it out. Cover with one-third of the raspberries, spread out evenly, again touching the sides of the bowl so the layer will be visible. Use a small sieve to dust the berries with half the icing sugar. Pour half the custard over the berries. Repeat the above set of layers again. Top with the third layer of cake, brush with the remaining syrup and top with the remaining berries, reserving a few raspberries for garnish. Cover and refrigerate while you whip the cream.

15. In a large bowl or in the bowl of a stand mixer fitted with a whisk attachment, whisk the cream on high just until stiff peaks form. Remove the trifle from the fridge, gently spoon the whipped cream over the berries and use an offset spatula to spread into an even layer. Garnish with more berries and refrigerate for at least 3 hours or overnight.

Note | The trifle can be made up to 24 hours ahead and leftovers can be kept, covered in the fridge, for up to 2 days.

DRINKS

Makes: 8 spoons
Dietary Notes: GF*, V

Hot Chocolate BROOMS

Brooms are ubiquitous in the wizarding world. For the films, these needed to be incredibly durable, so an aircraft grade titanium centre was covered by mahogany wood, then birch branches were added for the bristle head. Some brooms were customized for their character: Tonks's broom had multicoloured branches in the head; Arthur Weasley's had a bicycle basket on it. These wood-handled spoon 'brooms' have a 'bristle head' of milk chocolate, cocoa and sugar that creates a warming drink you can customize with crushed peppermints, mini marshmallows or whipped cream.

> 'That's not just any broomstick, Harry. It's a Nimbus 2000!'
>
> —Ron Weasley,
> *Harry Potter and the Philosopher's Stone*

INGREDIENTS

- 320g milk chocolate chips
- 50g unsweetened cocoa powder
- 2½ tablespoons caster sugar
- 2 tablespoons whipping cream
- 240ml very hot milk or non-diary alternative, to serve
- 8 flat-handled wooden spoons

1. Line a baking tray with parchment paper.
2. In a microwave-safe bowl, melt half the chocolate chips in 30-second bursts, stirring until melted. Add the cocoa powder, sugar and cream and stir until combined and a thick paste forms.
3. Mould about 2 tablespoons of the mixture around the bowl of each of the wooden spoons, creating a broom shape. Press the shape against the baking tray to create a flat, stable bottom. Refrigerate for 20 minutes.
4. Melt the remaining chocolate chips as above. Remove the brooms from the fridge and dip each one in the melted chocolate, using an offset spatula to make sure the whole broom is covered and sealed to the spoon handle. Use the tines of a fork to drag the chocolate and create the broom's texture. Place back on the baking tray, standing upright, and repeat with the remaining spoons. Chill for 10 minutes or until set.
5. To serve, pour 240ml very hot milk, or non-dairy beverage of choice, into a mug. Place a broom in the mug, leave to stand for 2 minutes and then stir!
6. Make sure to have plenty of toppings on hand, such as mini marshmallows, peppermint chips and whipped cream.
7. The brooms can be stored in an airtight container for up to 2 weeks or packaged in cellophane bags for gift giving. If desired, use a fine tip pen to write on the broom handles, personalize with the names of the recipients, Nimbus 2000, Nimbus 2001, Firebolt or Quidditch World Cup.

Makes: 4 servings
Dietary Notes: GF, V, V+*

Hogwarts
PUNCH

In *Harry Potter and the Goblet of Fire*, one thing many of the students look forward to during the Triwizard Tournament is the Yule Ball that takes place over the Christmas holiday. Tables were set with food and beverages, the drinks served from two cauldron-shaped punch bowls that bracketed an icy centrepiece. Beverages were also available in long-necked bottles etched with snowflakes that contained one of four pastel-coloured liquids representing Hogwarts' four houses. This Hogwarts punch honours the two winners of the tournament — Hufflepuff Cedric Diggory and Gryffindor Harry Potter — with its yellow golden hue. This, Durmstrang Punch (see page 141) and Beauxbatons Punch (see page 143) are small batches meant to be served as a trio to create twelve servings. They are easily doubled or even tripled to create larger batches.

INGREDIENTS

- 1 litre lemonade
- 120ml apricot nectar
- 3—4 sprigs fresh thyme, plus more for garnish
- 2 tablespoons honey
- ½ lemon, thinly sliced for garnish
- ¼ teaspoon gold lustre dust (optional)

1. In a medium saucepan, combine the lemonade, apricot nectar, thyme and honey over medium heat. Bring to a low boil, remove from the heat and leave to steep for 30 minutes. Strain through a fine-mesh sieve into a wide mouth measuring jug and chill until serving.

2. To serve, pour into a large jug or punch bowl. Stir in the lustre dust, if using, and float the lemon slices and thyme sprigs in the punch.

Note | For a vegan option, use agave instead of honey.

> 'I just wondered if maybe you wanted to go to the ball with me?'
>
> —Harry Potter to Cho Chang,
> *Harry Potter and the Goblet of Fire*

Durmstrang PUNCH

Makes: 4 servings
Dietary Notes: GF, V, V+

Any punch that would represent Durmstrang Institute would need to be fiery, bringing to mind the fire-breathers that announce the entrance of these students into the Great Hall for the Triwizard Tournament. The colour red is also prominent on their military-style uniforms, which bear the double-headed eagle, the symbol for the school. And for the Yule Ball, the Durmstrang men stood out in bright red coats with talon-shaped fasteners and a fur-lined half cape that unfurled as they swung their partners around in the dance. With black peppercorns and ginger for zing, and cherry and apple juices for sweetness, this punch will make you flip like the proud sons of Durmstrang.

> 'And now our friends from the North — please greet the proud sons of Durmstrang.'
>
> —Albus Dumbledore,
> *Harry Potter and the Goblet of Fire*

INGREDIENTS

- 480ml apple juice
- 1 bay leaf
- One 7.5-cm piece of fresh ginger, peeled and thinly sliced
- 1 tablespoon black peppercorns
- 480ml unsweetened cherry juice
- ¼ teaspoon silver lustre dust (optional)
- Fresh bay leaves, for garnish (optional)

1. In a medium saucepan over medium heat, combine the apple juice, bay leaf, ginger slices and peppercorns. Bring to the boil and then remove from the heat and leave to steep for about 30 minutes. Strain through a fine-mesh sieve into a measuring jug.
2. Combine the infused apple juice with the cherry juice in a measuring jug and chill until ready to serve.
3. To serve, pour into a large jug or punch bowl and garnish with fresh bay leaves, if using. Stir in the lustre dust, if using.

Note | This punch is also delicious served warm. These are small batch punches meant to be served as a trio to create 12 servings. They are easily doubled or even tripled to create larger batches.

Beauxbatons PUNCH

Makes: 4 Servings
Dietary Notes: GF, V, V+

The lovely ladies of Beauxbatons Academy have a chic nature that balances with the steel in their spines. With the same style, this fragrant punch combines the calming earthy undertones of lavender with the crispness of sparkling white grape juice for a refreshing drink that epitomizes the sophisticated students. Costume designer Jany Temime, being French herself, chose the classic 'French blue' colour for the Beauxbatons girls' outfits, but for the Yule Ball, she wanted something that better reflected the culture and couture of her country. To show unity among the students, the Beauxbatons were dressed in grey-blue gowns, with thirty metres of chiffon in Fleur Delacour's gown alone!

INGREDIENTS

- 100g caster sugar
- 2 teaspoons dried culinary lavender
- 1–2 drops light blue food colouring
- ¼ teaspoon periwinkle blue lustre dust (optional)
- 1 litre sparkling white grape juice, chilled
- Fresh lavender sprigs, for garnish (optional)

1. In a small saucepan, over medium heat, bring the sugar and 240ml water to the boil, stirring until the sugar is completely dissolved. Remove from the heat and stir in the lavender. Leave to steep for 30 minutes.

2. Strain through a fine-mesh sieve into a measuring jug, add the food colouring and lustre dust, if using. Store in an airtight container in the fridge until ready to serve.

3. To serve, combine the lavender syrup and the sparkling grape juice, by gently stirring them into a large jug or punch bowl. Float lavender sprigs in the punch, if using.

> 'Please join me in welcoming the lovely ladies of Beauxbatons Academy of Magic …'
>
> —Albus Dumbledore,
> *Harry Potter and the Goblet of Fire*

Note | These are small batch punches meant to be served as a trio to create 12 servings. They are easily doubled or even tripled to create larger batches.

Makes: 4 servings
Dietary Notes: GF, V, V+

Professor Trelawney's
FORTIFIED EARL GREY TEA

Tessomancy is the art of reading tea leaves, which is the first lesson Professor Sybill Trelawney teaches in her third years' initial Divination class. Ron interprets Harry's tea leaves as that he will suffer, but he'll be happy about it. When Trelawney looks at it, she sees the 'Grim', an omen of death. Of course, she sees something negative in every cup she views. This drink is nothing but positives: the bold flavour of Earl Grey tea, a lemony simple syrup and the fortification of a nice dry gin.

> 'Broaden your mind!'
>
> —Sybill Trelawney,
> *Harry Potter and the Prisoner of Azkaban*

INGREDIENTS

For the Lemon Simple Syrup
3 lemons
200g caster sugar

For the Tea
2 Earl Grey tea bags

120ml lemon simple syrup
240ml fresh squeezed lemon juice
240ml gin
4 lemon slices, for garnish

1. **To make the lemon simple syrup:** Use a vegetable peeler or paring knife to remove the rind from the lemons, leaving behind as much pith as possible. Reserve the lemons for juicing.
2. Add the lemon rind to a small saucepan with 240ml water and the sugar. Bring to the boil over medium heat and stir for about 1 minute until the sugar is completely dissolved. Remove from the heat, leave to cool and store in an airtight container in the fridge for up to 1 week.
3. **To make the tea:** In a heatproof measuring jug or mug, combine the tea bags with 240ml boiling water and leave to steep for 6 minutes. Remove the tea bags and chill the tea in the fridge until serving.
4. To serve, fill a jug halfway with ice, add the tea, lemon simple syrup, lemon juice and gin.
5. Stir until well chilled, then pour through a sieve into tea cups or glasses. Garnish with a lemon slice.

Makes: 8 servings
Dietary Notes: GF, V, V+

Cast a Christmas Spell
SPICED CIDER

Spiced cider is a classic holiday beverage, served all through the Christmas season. Its origins have been thought to trace back to another drink known as wassail, made from roasted apples and sung about in a popular Christmas carol. Ghostly carolers sing a Hogwarts ode to the holiday, called 'Ring the Hogwarts Bell', in *Harry Potter and the Philosopher's Stone*. Dressed in Dickensian-type outfits, they fill the halls with this song as students leave for the holiday. This hot and fruity spiced cider would be the perfect drink to end any winter's day, whether you're carolling or just Christmas-ing.

> 'Merry Christmas,
> Merry Christmas
>
> Ring the Hogwarts bell!
>
> Merry Christmas,
> Merry Christmas
>
> Cast a Christmas spell!'
>
> —Hogwarts Ghostly Carolers,
> *Harry Potter and the Philosopher's Stone*

Note | This recipe can easily be doubled for a larger crowd. Slow cookers are ideal for mulled drinks because they cook at a low and constant temperature.

INGREDIENTS

- 2 apples
- 2 oranges
- 1 tablespoon whole cloves
- 2 litres unfiltered apple cider
- 4 tablespoons brown sugar
- 4 cinnamon sticks
- 2 whole star anise
- ⅛ teaspoon nutmeg

1. Slice one of the apples into thin round slices and gently remove the pips. Reserve the second apple for garnish.
2. Slice one orange in half lengthways, then slice each half into thin slices. Reserve the second orange for garnish.
3. Poke the cloves into the end slices of orange so they can be easily removed from the mixture, or place them in a tea infuser.
4. **Slow cooker method:** Add the cider, sugar, sliced apple, sliced orange, cloves, cinnamon, star anise and nutmeg to the slow cooker and heat for 1–1½ hours on low, stirring halfway through.
5. **Stove top method:** Add 1 litre of the cider and the sugar to a large saucepan over medium-low heat. Cook, stirring occasionally, until the sugar dissolves and the cider is at a low boil. Lower the heat to low and add the remaining cider, sliced apple, sliced orange, cloves, cinnamon, star anise and nutmeg. Bring back to a simmer over low heat and cook for 30–45 minutes. Turn off the heat, stir and leave to sit for 10–15 minutes.
6. Serve the cider warm in mugs with fresh fruit sliced as above. Add one piece each to the mugs.
7. Cider can be stored in an airtight container in the fridge for 1–2 days. Be sure to remove the fruit and whole spices before storing, so the spice level does not become too strong and fruit does not ferment. Reheat in the slow cooker or in a large pan over medium heat before serving.

Makes: 2 servings
Dietary Notes: GF, V, V+

HAIR OF THE CAT

To discover the identity of the Heir of Slytherin, who has unleashed the deadly Basilisk upon Muggle-borns at Hogwarts in *Harry Potter and the Chamber of Secrets*, Hermione concocts Polyjuice Potion for transformations using hairs from Crabbe and Goyle that will allow Harry and Ron to enter the Slytherin dormitory. Hermione, regrettably, took cat hairs off Slytherin Millicent Bulstrode's robes and transformed into a human/cat hybrid, so she could not go. As the special effects team wanted the potion to look and taste as disgusting as possible, it was made of lumps of vegetable and different coloured edible dyes, and the drink was served cold to garner a real reaction from the actors. This drink, inspired by that moment, blends tropical kiwis, lime and coconut that will give the real reaction of delight to this exotic brew.

INGREDIENTS

- 2 ripe kiwis
- 480ml coconut water, chilled
- 2 teaspoons chia seeds
- 1 lime
- ⅛ teaspoon green lustre dust (optional)
- 4 tablespoons shredded coconut, toasted

1. Peel and core the kiwis and add the flesh to a blender. Add the coconut water and blend on high until the kiwi is puréed. Transfer the mixture to an airtight container and add the chia seeds, juice of half the lime and lustre dust, if using. Stir to combine. Cover and refrigerate for 15–20 minutes or until thickened.
2. Just before serving, cut the remaining lime half in half and use the quarters to wet the rims of two glasses.
3. Pour the toasted coconut onto a shallow plate and twist the rims of the glasses in the coconut to coat.
4. Split the mixture between the 2 glasses and serve immediately.

> 'Look at my face.'
> 'Look at your tail!'
>
> —Hermione Granger and Ron Weasley,
> *Harry Potter and the Chamber of Secrets*

Makes: 6 servings
Dietary Notes: GF, V, V+*

Magical
MULLED WINE

To mull something means to heat it, sweeten it and flavour it with spices, something revellers in the British Isles have been doing for centuries. This heartening drink features the sweetness of oranges and honey, the liquorice-y tang of star anise and a generous dollop of brandy for heat. It not only tastes good, but its colours also look great at any Christmas party. Mead was historically created by the Romans who occupied the colder European regions; not only did it warm them up, it had health benefits as well due to the fruits and spices. Mulled wine is very similar to mead, a bottle of which Horace Slughorn shares with Harry and Ron, but they discover it has been poisoned when Ron falls ill. Mulled wine would have been much healthier!

> 'Here, old boy. Bottom's up!'
> —Horace Slughorn,
> *Harry Potter and the Half-Blood Prince*

INGREDIENTS

- 3 clementine oranges
- 1 tablespoon whole cloves
- One 750-ml bottle of dry red wine
- 240ml orange juice
- 140g honey
- 2 tablespoons brown sugar
- 4 cinnamon sticks
- 2 whole star anise
- 1 bay leaf
- ⅛ teaspoon allspice
- 60ml brandy (optional)

1. Slice two of the clementines into three thick slices each. Reserve the remaining clementine for garnish.
2. Poke the cloves into the ends of the oranges so they can be removed from the mixture easily, or place in a tea infuser.
3. **Slow cooker method:** Add the wine, sliced oranges, orange juice, honey, brown sugar, cinnamon, star anise, bay leaf, allspice and brandy, if using, and stir gently to combine. Cook on low for 1½ hours. Use a slotted spoon to remove the oranges and whole spices.
4. **Stove top method:** In a large saucepan over medium heat, add the orange juice, honey and sugar and bring to a low boil until the sugar and honey dissolve. Add the wine, oranges, cinnamon, star anise, bay leaf, allspice and brandy, if using. Bring back to a simmer, then lower the heat to low and cook for 30 minutes. Use a slotted spoon to remove the oranges and whole spices.
5. Serve hot in mugs with fresh clementine sliced rounds floating in each mug.
6. Mulled wine can be stored in an airtight container in the fridge for 1—2 days. Be sure to remove the oranges and whole spices before storing, so the spice level does not become too strong and fruit does not ferment. Gently reheat in the slow cooker or in a large pan over medium-low heat, until desired temperature, before serving, but do not re-boil.

Note | For a vegan version, swap the honey for agave. The spices and fruit will be adding so much flavour that an expensive wine is not necessary. Inexpensive Cabernet, Zinfandel or Malbec is ideal.

Mistletoe COCKTAIL

Makes: 2 servings
Dietary Notes: GF, V, V+

Harry Potter experiences his first kiss with Cho Chang after the students in Dumbledore's Army leave for the Christmas holiday in *Harry Potter and the Order of the Phoenix*. He's had a crush on her for a while, and the two finally express their feelings when Cho points out that they're standing underneath a sprig of mistletoe. Both Daniel Radcliffe and Katie Leung were nervous before the scene was filmed. Radcliffe remembers 'lots of courtesy gum chewing that day'. The edible mint leaves in this cocktail represent the inedible mistletoe, and ought to ensure that any smooch should be a success.

INGREDIENTS

- 5–6 mint leaves, plus more for garnish
- 120ml coconut milk
- 30ml simple syrup, plus more for garnish
- 60ml lime juice
- 120ml white rum
- 60ml coconut water
- 1 tablespoon caster sugar, for garnish

1. In a cocktail shaker, muddle together the mint, coconut milk and simple syrup. Add 5–6 ice cubes to the cocktail shaker and top off with the lime juice, rum and coconut water.
2. Fill 2 highball glasses halfway with ice.
3. Shake until the cocktail shaker is frosted over. Strain between the two glasses. Garnish with sugared mint leaves (see note).

Note | To make sugared mint leaves, mix 1 teaspoon simple syrup with 1 teaspoon water until thoroughly combined. Use a pastry brush to apply a very thin layer of simple syrup mixture onto the leaves of two short mint sprigs. Sprinkle with sugar and set aside on a plate to dry until needed. To garnish the cocktail, place a cocktail stick across the top of the glass and hang the sugared mint upside down over the cocktail stick, like mistletoe.

> 'Mistletoe.'
>
> 'Probably full of Nargles, though.'
>
> —Cho Chang and Harry Potter, *Harry Potter and the Order of the Phoenix*

PUMPKIN FIZZ

Makes: 1 serving
Dietary Notes: V, GF

Pumpkins are prevalent in the wizarding world: Pumpkin Juice (a popular drink among the Hogwarts students) and pumpkins that hang over the tables of the Great Hall at Halloween. There's a pumpkin patch next to Hagrid's hut, and there are even pumpkin-shaped chocolate cakes, served at the welcoming feast for the Triwizard Tournament. Interestingly, a few of the prop pumpkins in Hagrid's pumpkin patch were used to make the moulds for the chocolate cakes. The sweetness of apple juice combines with the spicy kicks of pumpkin butter and gingery bubbles for a lip-smacking iced fizzy drink.

> 'You'll find no small glasses in this house.'
>
> —Rubeus Hagrid,
> *Harry Potter and the Prisoner of Azkaban*

INGREDIENTS

For the Pumpkin Butter
1.4kg butternut squash or pumpkin
240ml apple juice
2 tablespoons bourbon or vanilla extract
200g dark brown sugar
1 teaspoon ground cinnamon
¼ teaspoon ground clove

For the Pumpkin Fizz
3 tablespoons apple juice
2 tablespoons pumpkin butter (or shop-bought)
180—240ml ginger beer or ginger ale

Speciality Tools
Eight 120-ml or four 240-ml jars

1. **To make the pumpkin butter:** Have ready eight 120-ml or four 240-ml jars with tight-fitting lids, well washed or sterilized. Preheat the oven to 160°C Fan/180°C/Gas 4.

2. Halve each squash and scoop out the seeds and stringy pulp. Cut the stem end off and discard it.

3. Pour 120ml of the apple juice with 120ml water into a roasting pan. Place the squash pieces, cut side down, in the pan and roast for 45—50 minutes, or until very tender when poked with a fork.

4. Leave the squash to cool for 10 minutes, then use a fork and spoon to scrape the flesh from the skin.

5. Place all the flesh and the cooking liquid in a large heavy-based saucepan. Discard the skin.

6. Add the remaining apple juice, the bourbon, brown sugar, cinnamon and clove. Place over medium heat and cook, stirring, for about 10 minutes until the mixture begins to bubble. Turn the heat down to low, cover partially and simmer for 20—25 minutes, or until the mixture clings to a spoon for several seconds before falling back in the pan.

7. Remove from the heat and use a handheld blender to purée into a smooth texture. Immediately fill the clean jars and seal with tight-fitting lids. Leave to cool to room temperature and then refrigerate. The pumpkin butter will store in the fridge for up to 3 weeks.

8. **To make the fizz:** In a tall glass, mix the apple juice and pumpkin butter together until smooth. Fill the glass with ice and top off with ginger beer or ginger ale. Stir gently to combine or serve layered, with a spoon or straw.

Makes: 240ml of syrup
Dietary Notes: GF, V, V+

Black Lake
SIMPLE SYRUP

A simple syrup sweetens any beverage by the simple act of combining equal parts sugar and water, heating it so the sugar dissolves, and then adding it to iced drinks or cocktails. It can also be flavoured by adding other ingredients, such as, with this Black Lake-inspired version, black cocoa powder. The Black Lake is aptly named — it's hard to see anything under its murky waters, as Harry learns during the second task of the Triwizard Tournament in *Harry Potter and the Goblet of Fire*. Black Lake Simple Syrup can be mixed with sparkling wine for a dark mimosa, added to ginger ale or used to create a Black and Orange (see page 155). This simple syrup will make any drink darker and sweeter, simply.

INGREDIENTS

200g caster sugar

1 tablespoon black cocoa powder

1. In a small saucepan over medium-high heat, combine the sugar with 240ml water. Bring to the boil, stirring continuously, for about 1 minute until all the sugar is dissolved.
2. Remove from the heat, leave to cool for 15 minutes and whisk in the cocoa powder until the mixture is smooth and no lumps remain. Keep in an airtight container in the fridge for up to 1 week.

BLACK AND ORANGE

Makes: 4 servings
Dietary Notes: GF, V, V+

A Black and Tan is a popular cocktail that combines a dark and a light beer, which separates due to the different densities in the drinks. This 'black and orange' version gives it a wizarding twist, layering in the sweet Black Lake Simple Syrup (see page 154) and full-bodied piquancy of a Pumpkin Fizz.

> 'Myrtle, there aren't merpeople in the Black Lake are there?'
>
> —Harry Potter,
> *Harry Potter and the Goblet of Fire*

INGREDIENTS

- 2 tablespoons Black Lake Simple Syrup (see page 154)
- 3 tablespoons apple juice
- 2 tablespoons pumpkin butter (see page 153)
- 180–240ml ginger beer or ale

1. Pour the simple syrup into the bottom of a large glass, being careful not to get it on the side.
2. In a small bowl, combine the apple juice and pumpkin butter together until smooth.
3. Fill the glass with ice and pour the apple juice mixture over it. Let the layers settle a minute and then top with ginger beer or ginger ale by slowly pouring it over the back of a spoon. Serve immediately with a spoon or straw for stirring.

THE GREY LADY

Makes: 1 serving
Dietary Notes: GF

In *Harry Potter and the Deathly Hallows — Part 2*, it was learned that the ghost of Ravenclaw house, the Grey Lady, was actually the daughter of Rowena Ravenclaw. Rowena, the Ravenclaw house founder, wore a diadem that Voldemort turned into a Horcrux. The diadem, designed by Miraphora Mina, features the Ravenclaw eagle in blue stones surrounded by white drops and the Ravenclaw house motto. This drink visually references the sparkle of the Diadem with a glistening sugar rim and the ghostly presence of the Grey Lady with a bluish gray liquid colour.

> 'Wit beyond measure is man's greatest treasure.'
>
> —Ravenclaw house motto

INGREDIENTS

For the Blue Simple Syrup
200g caster sugar
1 tablespoon butterfly pea flowers

For the Drink
2 tablespoons dark blue sanding sugar
½ tablespoon blue simple syrup
3 blackberries
1 teaspoon meringue powder
60ml vodka
30ml St. Germain or elderflower liqueur

Speciality Tools
Coupe glass

1. **To make the blue simple syrup:** In a small saucepan combine the sugar with 240ml water and bring to the boil over medium-high heat. Stir continuously until the sugar is completely dissolved. Remove from the heat, stir in the flowers and allow to steep for about 1 hour until completely cool. Strain through a fine-mesh sieve into an airtight container and store the syrup in the fridge for up to 1 week.

2. **To make the drink:** Place the sanding sugar in a shallow dish. Rim the cocktail glass with a bit of simple syrup and place the glass, rim edge down, in the sugar. Give it a twist until the entire rim is covered in sugar. Press one blackberry against the edge of the glass to hold.

3. Muddle the remaining two blackberries and blue simple syrup in the bottom of a cocktail shaker. Add the meringue powder, vodka and St. Germain. Add a few ice cubes, leaving plenty of room to create froth. Shake vigorously until the cocktail shaker frosts over and strain into the coupe glass. Serve immediately.

Note | Food colouring can be used instead of the butterfly pea flowers in the blue simple syrup, but it does not have the same colour changing magic as the butterfly pea flower and will affect the colour of your cocktail.

HARRY POTTER
HOLIDAY-THEMED PARTIES

'On Christmas Eve night, we and our guests gather in the Great Hall for a night of well-mannered frivolity.'

—Minerva McGonagall, *Harry Potter and the Goblet of Fire*

PARTY PLANNING
AND SUGGESTED MENUS

Is there anything better than gathering friends and family for a party with great food and drink, lively conversation and bright and colourful decorations? Well, we think there is — when the party is themed to the amazing wizarding world films that feature Harry Potter, Ron Weasley and Hermione Granger, among many fascinating witches and wizards.

But festive parties don't just appear with a wave of your wand. Every party takes time, hard work and attention to detail to make it unique and memorable, for both the party guests and the party giver. The filmmakers served 450 students in the Welcome Feast in *Harry Potter and the Philosopher's Stone*, but for your first time hosting a wizarding bash, you might want to aim for a smaller number of guests. The type of party you host can be an elaborate dance party like the Yule Ball in *Harry Potter and the Goblet of Fire* or a cozy cocktail party similar to the Slug Club Christmas gathering in *Harry Potter and the Half-Blood Prince*.

There's a lot to consider when planning a party, especially your table scape, including dinnerware, linens, serving dishes, cutlery and table covers. Hogwarts uses gold plates and flatware at all its mealtimes. Set out place cards if you'd like and add a centrepiece or two to the table. Horace Slughorn used red lanterns, and the Weasleys had Christmas crackers and holiday cards strewn around Grimmauld Place during their Christmas there.

Setting the scene is important and decorations are key: Trees, ornaments, garlands and twinkling lights will bring magic to your get-together. You can decorate your Christmas tree with a gold star or a gold gnome as the topper, and feature large and small gold stars, crescent moons, long-tailed partridges and glittering orbs similar to the ones Professor Flitwick levitated onto the Great Hall's trees using *Wingardium Leviosa*. Or decorate the tree in your house colours: in Harry's first year, Gryffindor's Christmas tree featured gold Christmas crackers (an English Christmas tradition) and miniature, red-coloured gift boxes.

If you're not able to have a tree, you can drape bowers of evergreen branches on shelves or over doors and decorate them with golden pine cones or other ornaments. You can also hang wreaths from doors or the walls. The smell of pine or fir will add to the Christmas ambience of your party. Stream a crackling fireplace on your TV or any monitor if you don't have a fireplace yourself and hang some mistletoe in the room (just watch out for Nargles!).

Food really sets the flavour of any party, and a party with a specific theme such as 'Christmas in the Wizarding World' lends itself to an iconic menu. Traditional fare features roast meats and vegetables, or you can have savoury seafood or curries. Or, like the Welcome Feast for the Triwizard Tournament in *Harry Potter and the Goblet of Fire*, you can serve only desserts! Hors d'oeuvres can range from the sweet to the salty, and there's nothing like a Hot Chocolate Broom or Magical Mulled Wine in the chilly season.

Festive activities can include carolling, exchanging presents, hanging Christmas cards or paper snowflakes in a red-and-gold or silver-and-green twisted garland around your living space, or making Christmas crackers and spirals of gold tinsel with which you can decorate the tree.

You can even put together your own version of the Yule Ball, with a program of events, such as a demonstration of wand moves. Dancing would be in order; you can distribute a card before the event with a dance tutorial (make sure you label right and left feet correctly!). The Yule Ball seen in *Harry Potter and the Goblet of Fire* featured silver plates and flatware and crystal-cut glasses; tablecloths, chairs and everything else in the room was draped in silver fabric. Punch can be served in a cauldron-shaped bowl, and fake snow can be sprayed on trees or pine boughs. Be sure to 'dress to impress', as is written on the original Yule Ball invitation. (Design your own dress robes but avoid any advice on this from Ron's Great-Aunt Tessie!)

Celebrate a wizarding world Christmas at any time of the year. Spray fake removable snow on your windows and wear your wool house scarf inside. Play carols in the background while you cook mouthwatering feasts and bake sumptuous desserts. Any time is the right time to have a happy Christmas.

White Erumpent
GIFT EXCHANGE

A White Elephant is a gift exchange where participants can swap around gifts they pull out of a sack, hoping to walk away with the best one in the bag, rather than the worst, which is referred to as the white elephant. Those in the wizarding world might call it a White Erumpent Gift Exchange. In this version, everyone brings a Harry Potter-themed gift and the host puts a Holiday Fruitcake they've made to act as the White Erumpent. First, everyone draws a number, and the gifts are chosen in that order. You can either choose a new gift from the bag, or 'steal' a gift from someone who has gone before. Note however that a gift can only be stolen once per round. But once a gift has been passed between 3 people, the third owner gets to keep the gift and it can no longer be stolen. The magic here is that whoever gets the fruitcake will be the winner because it will be delicious!

Yule Ball
PARTY MENU

Hogwarts students receive an invitation requesting the pleasure of their company to celebrate Christmas and the Triwizard Tournament at the Yule Ball, where beverages and a Yule Feast are served, a Witch and Wizard of the Ball are announced, and there's a Yule Parade of Wand Skills. This menu will complement a 'night of well-mannered frivolity' with colourful punches, succulent fish dishes and a creamy, fruity layered confection.

Bubbling Cauldron Bites... 25

Yule Ball Prawn Cocktail.. 29

Golden Egg Meat Pies... 71

Beauxbatons French Fish... 80

Triwizard Trifle 131

Hogwarts, Durmstrang
and Beauxbatons Punches........................ 139, 141, 143

Slug Club
COCKTAIL PARTY MENU

Professor Horace Slughorn hosts several parties during the events of *Harry Potter and the Half-Blood Prince*. At his Christmas party, he gathers together the most recent Slug Club members with those witches and wizards he's stayed in touch with over the years. A cocktail party is a wonderful occasion for new friends and old to meet and enjoy an intimate holiday gathering. There's a wide variety of tastes and textures in this suggested menu; there are nutty and fruity, as well as fiery and cool selections, all of which will charm your guests.

Slug Club Christmas Party Spiced Nuts.................. 23
Swedish Short-Snout's Steak Tartare..................... 27
Slughorn's Appetizer Roll-Ups 31
Famous Fire-Eaters Beef Skewers........................... 63
Butterscotch Ice Cream Pie 109
Professor Flitwick's Figgy Pudding........................ 128
Hair of the Cat 147
Pumpkin Fizz 153

MOVIE NIGHT
Around the Fire Menu

On a cold winter's night, there's nothing better than getting together to watch a favourite movie or two with film fans and companions. This Movie Night around the Fire menu is filled with entertaining comfort food that will warm viewers from head to toe even if there isn't a fireplace nearby. A visit to Hogwarts by watching the Harry Potter films can easily provide a substitute, from the huge fireplace in the Gryffindor common room to the blazing fire and flambeaux in the Great Hall of Hogwarts.

Hagrid's One-Pot Pumpkin Stew *36*

Leaky Cauldron's Roasted Tomato Soup with Marmite Grilled Cheese Sandwich *38*

Golden Snitch Popcorn Balls *87*

Every Flavour Cake Pops *91*

Hot Chocolate Brooms *137*

Cast a Christmas Spell Spiced Cider *145*

Grimmauld Place
CHRISTMAS EVE MENU

Christmas Eve is a time of great fun and anticipation — who will be there, what stories will everyone tell, and what will my presents be tomorrow? (If you're a Weasley, it's pretty certain you'll get something knitted from Molly!) It's a good idea to have a hearty, grounding menu for the eve before the Christmas holiday and this very special dinner offers a nod towards tradition and a wink (as Sirius did to Harry) at the future.

Sprout's Superior Sprouts	45
Grimmauld Place Dinner Rolls	48
Sirius Black Hearth Potatoes	51
Hogwarts Yorkshire Pudding	55
Christmas Eve Beef Roast	74
Snowy Burrow Cake	103
Magical Mulled Wine	149

CHRISTMAS DAY MENU

If there is one thing Muggles and wizards have in common, it's the love of being with family and friends to celebrate Christmas. During this time, Hogwarts is decorated with fragrant trees and wreaths, thoughtful presents are exchanged, and everyone gathers together around the table to feast on crisp greens, juicy meats and hearty breads. And then there's always a spectacular dessert that heightens the sweetness of the holiday. A Christmas Day menu such as this one is sure to make for magical merriment.

Nicolas Flamel Vichyssoise Soup 34

The Burrow Welcome Wreath 43

Greenhouse Greens Salad.. 59

Christmas Day Rack of Lamb 73
or Grimmauld Place Roast Turkey Feast 77

Great Hall Floating Candle Cake 111

Mistletoe Cocktail.. 150

BOXING DAY
Get-Together Menu

Boxing Day is the day after Christmas, a perfect time to visit those who had their own family or friends Christmas feasts and exchange gifts. Gifts that come in boxes, of course, but you can also get together and gift those you care about with an array of giftable treats. These recipes are a gift as well — they use up any leftovers from Christmas Day, are great for a brunch-type celebration and are tremendously tasty.

Restricted Section Puff Pastry Books 10

Snape's Bubble and Squeak........................ 13

The Burrow Welcome Wreath 43

Hagrid's Pumpkin Seed Brittle 89

**Professor Trelawney's
Fortified Earl Grey Tea** 144

GLOSSARY

Deglaze: Deglazing is adding liquid, usually wine or stock, to a hot pan to release all the caramelized food from the pan. These caramelized bits, called fond, are full of flavour and should not be left behind. Deglazing is often the first step in making a delicious sauce.

Egg Wash: Whisk together 1 egg and 1 tablespoon water until light and foamy. Use a pastry brush to apply when the recipe requires.

High-Heat vs. Nonstick Pans: Many recipes in the book call for high-heat pans. Typically, this would mean stainless steel, cast iron or enamelled cast iron. Stove temperatures are based on these types of cookware. If you are cooking with nonstick cookware, please make sure that you know the manufacturer's heat limits for your cookware. Most nonstick cookware should not be used at above medium heat on a stove and is not suitable for the oven. Cooking times may need to be adjusted to account for this.

Lustre Dust: This dust is a food-safe glitter that can be purchased online or in speciality baking departments. It can be mixed with clear alcohol to create a shimmery paint or brushed on dry.

Milk: The word milk in this book is always referring to dairy milk unless otherwise noted. In most cases any percentage of milk fat will do unless otherwise noted.

Peeling Ginger: The easiest way to peel fresh ginger is with a small spoon. Simply use the edge of the spoon to scrape away the peel. This keeps the ginger root intact, with less waste, and allows you to easily navigate all the bumps and lumps.

Salt: Feel free to use your salt of choice unless it has been noted in the recipe. Kosher salt is the one most commonly used throughout the book.

Silicone Baking Mat: Silicone baking mats can be used up to high temperatures in the oven and used in the freezer. They are very helpful in baking because you can easily roll dough out on them and then take them from prep station to chilling to oven without having to move dough. They are extremely nonstick and easy to clean.

Sumac: Made from ground berries of the sumac flower. It has a sour and slightly acidic taste and is most commonly used in Mediterranean and Middle Eastern cooking. It is great for dry rubs, marinades and even dressings. It adds a great punch of flavour and colour.

Vanilla Paste vs. Vanilla Extract: Vanilla bean paste can give you the strong vanilla flavour and the beautiful vanilla bean flecks without having to split and steep a vanilla bean. While it is more expensive than extract, there are recipes where it will really shine and elevate a dish. When it will make a wonderful addition to a dish it has been called out, but it can always be replaced with vanilla extract with a 1-for-1 swap out.

DIETARY CONSIDERATIONS

Key | GF: Gluten Free | V: Vegetarian V+: Vegan
V*: Easily made vegetarian | V+*: Easily made vegan
GF*: Easily made gluten free

Breakfasts
Restricted Section Puff Pastry Books	V
Granola Breakfast of Triwizard Champions	GF*, V, V+*
Snape's Bubble and Squeak	GF, V*
Neville's Toad in the Hole	
The Chosen One Toast Lightning Bolts with Coddled Egg	GF*, V

Soups & Starters
Slug Club Christmas Party Spiced Nuts	GF, V
Bubbling Cauldron Bites	GF, V
Swedish Short-Snout's Steak Tartare	GF*
Yule Ball Prawn Cocktail	GF
Slughorn's Appetizer Roll-Ups	GF, V*, V+*
Nicolas Flamel Vichyssoise Soup	GF, V
Hagrid's One-Pot Pumpkin Stew	GF, V, V+
Leaky Cauldron's Roasted Tomato Soup with Marmite Grilled Cheese	GF*, V, V+*

Breads & Sides
The Burrow Welcome Wreath	V
Sprout's Superior Sprouts	GF
Grimmauld Place Dinner Rolls	V
Sirius Black Hearth Potatoes	GF, V, V+*
Weasley Sweater Focaccia	V, V+
Hogwarts Yorkshire Pudding	V*

Mains
Greenhouse Greens Salad	GF, V, V+*
Madam Pomfrey's Hospitality Shepherd's Pie	GF, V
Famous Fire Eaters Spicy Beef Skewers	GF
Marauder's Map Tart	
Golden Egg Meat Pies	
Christmas Eve Beef Roast	GF
Christmas Day Rack of Lamb	GF
Grimmauld Place Roast Turkey Feast	GF*
Beauxbatons French Fish	GF
Yule Ball English Fish Pie	GF

Desserts
Golden Snitch Popcorn Balls	GF, V*
Hagrid's Pumpkin Seed Brittle	GF, V
Every Flavour Cake Pops	V
Mini Mincemeat Tarts	V
Great Hall Holiday Fruitcake	V
Harry's Favourite Treacle Tart	V
Snowy Burrow Cake	V
Sleepy Cupcakes	V
Great Hall Floating Candle Cake	V
Wizard Chess Pie	V
Butterscotch Ice Cream Pie	GF, V
'I'm Sorry, Neville' Biscuit Pops	V
Common Room Jam Sandwich Biscuits	V
Shortbread Christmas Biscuits	V
Golden Trio Biscuits	V
Professor Trelawney's Pots de Créme	GF, V
Hogsmeade Invisible Snowballs	V
Flitwick's Christmas Figgy Pudding	V
Butterscotch Ice Cream	GF, V
Triwizard Trifle	V

Drinks
Hot Chocolate Brooms	GF*, V
Hogwarts Punch	GF, V, V+*
Durmstrang Punch	GF, V, V+
Beauxbatons Punch	GF, V, V+
Cast a Christmas Spell Spiced Cider	GF, V, V+
Professor Trelawney's Fortified Earl Grey Tea	GF, V, V+
Hair of the Cat	GF, V, V+
Magical Mulled Wine	GF, V, V+*
Mistletoe Cocktail	GF, V, V+
Pumpkin Fizz	V
Black Lake Simple Syrup	GF, V, V+
Black and Orange	GF, V, V+
The Grey Lady	GF

First published in Great Britain in 2023 by

Greenfinch
An imprint of Quercus Editions Ltd
Carmelite House
50 Victoria Embankment
London EC4Y 0DZ

An Hachette UK company

Copyright © 2023 Warner Bros. Entertainment Inc. WIZARDING WORLD characters, names and related indicia are © & ™ Warner Bros. Entertainment Inc. WB SHIELD: TM & © WBEI. Publishing Rights © JKR. (s23)

All rights reserved. Published in the US by Insight Editions, San Rafael, California, in 2023.
No part of this book may be reproduced in any form without written permission from the publisher.

ISBN: 978-1-52943-473-6

Photographer: Ted Thomas
Prop and Food Stylist: Elena P. Craig
Assistant Food Stylist: Lauren Tedeschi
Assistant Food Stylist: Patricia Parrish
Photography Art Direction: Judy Wiatrek Trum
Interior Design: Mikaela Buck
Illustrations: Paula Hanback

Insight Editions, in association with Roots of Peace, will plant two trees for each tree used in the manufacturing of this book. Roots of Peace is an internationally renowned humanitarian organization dedicated to eradicating land mines worldwide and converting war-torn lands into productive farms and wildlife habitats. Roots of Peace will plant two million fruit and nut trees in Afghanistan and provide farmers there with the skills and support necessary for sustainable land use.

Manufactured in China by Insight Editions
10 9 8 7 6 5 4 3 2